English Allsorts

The EMC collection of ideas for English and Media classrooms

CD ROM
See inside cover

Acknowledgements

Barbara Bleiman, Jenny Grahame, Kate Oliver, Lucy Webster

Design and cover: Sam Sullivan
www.edition.co.uk

Illustrations: Rebecca Scambler

Printed by: Stephens and George Ltd

© English and Media Centre, 2008

18 Compton Terrace, London, N1 2UN

ISBN: 978-1-906101-01-5

Thanks to Ava Houris for reading and commenting on the text

Thanks also to the following publishers for giving permission for the use of copyright material:

The Guardian and John Crace for the 'Digested Read' of *Harry Potter and the Deathly Hallows*; David Higham Associates Ltd for 'I am the Song' by Charles Causley (*Collected Poems,* published by Pan Macmillan); Picador/Pan Macmillan for 'Introduction to Poetry' by Billy Collins; City Lights for 'Breakfast' ('Petit Dejeuner') by Jacques Prévert, trans. Lawrence Ferlinghetti (*Paroles*)

We have made every effort to obtain copyright permission. We would be grateful to hear from anyone we have been unable to contact.

Contents

Contents

English Allsorts

Alternative Index

Alternative Index

English Allsorts

Requires Little Preparation Or Few Resources

Mainly Group

Develops Thinking Skills

Role-Play And Simulation

Introduction

What is Allsorts?

English Allsorts is a compendium of strategies developed by advisory teachers at the English and Media Centre over the last 30 years. We have deliberately focused on strategies which are less generally known. Activities like hot-seating, balloon debates and freeze-frames have become staples of the English classroom, so we haven't included these. Of course, some of the strategies we have selected will be familiar to you, perhaps from EMC publications or courses; others we hope will be new to you.

Organisation

The book is organised into 14 main sections based loosely on the main areas of the English and Media curriculum, from essay and non-fiction writing to strategies for encouraging private reading and developing media literacy, plus a glossary of key media terms.

Inevitably many of the strategies could have been placed in several of the sections: 'Continuum Opinions', for example, is a strategy which not only develops Speaking and Listening but also develops students' ability to formulate and articulate arguments. 'And why not try...' cross references further strategies you may find useful.

The Alternative Index

Sometimes you may be looking for a strategy under a different kind of heading, for instance one that requires few resources or one that has links to the Citizenship curriculum or which develops argument skills. The Alternative Index on page 7 will help you locate appropriate strategies under a range of different possible headings.

The Strategies

Each strategy is presented in the same way with a table listing key information about the approach, an outline of the activity, variations and classroom tips. The key information in the

table includes: a brief overview of the strategy, what it is particularly good for, the age range it is most suitable for, timing and resources needed.

The outline of the activity is deliberately spare: these are strategies to be applied to the text or topic you are preparing to teach, rather than fully worked up resources to be taken into the classroom. 'Classroom tips' alerts you to particular issues you may need to be aware of before using it in the classroom, along with practical suggestions for ensuring the activity goes smoothly. 'Variations' includes both advice on differentiation and adapting the strategy for other age groups and suggests ways in which you could ring the changes. Many of the Media strategies offer variations specifically for use with students preparing to sit Media Studies examinations.

The CD ROM

English Allsorts is complemented by a free CD ROM. This CD ROM has two main folders:

● Allsorts

● EMC_Samples

'Allsorts' on the CD ROM provides exemplification of many of the strategies outlined in the book to give you a flavour of how they work in practice and of how they might be developed for the classroom, applied to specific texts and topics. Many of these are taken from EMC publications or course materials. 'Extra Allsorts' have been written for this publication and include grids, worksheets, classroom materials, further suggestions and examples.

'EMC_Samples' includes samples from every EMC publication currently in print (2007).

The CD ROM also includes the complete *Key Stage 3 Units* – 20 diverse and engaging units of work for 11-14 year-olds.

See 'What's on the CD ROM?' on page 149 for a full index of both 'Allsorts' and 'EMC_Samples'.

Speaking and Listening

And why not try...

You may also find the following activities useful:

1. Debate Around the Room

AGE	11-18
TIME	20-40 minutes
GROUPING	Individual and whole class
IN BRIEF	**A debating game for issues, texts or anything else where different viewpoints can be aired and argued about.**
GOOD FOR	• Developing confidence in speaking and listening. • Developing argument skills. • Debating a range of different interpretations on a text and finding evidence.
RESOURCES	Three large cards saying 'Agree', 'Disagree' and 'Undecided'; a controversial statement about the text or topic being studied.
ON CD ROM	*Great Expectations – an EMC Study Guide; Talk on the Box; Studying the World's Wife*

Activity

■ Put the three notices 'Agree', 'Disagree' and 'Undecided' up in different corners of the classroom.

■ Write a controversial statement up on the whiteboard, flipchart or interactive whiteboard.

■ In silence, each student thinks about their view on the statement, perhaps jotting down a few reasons for their decision.

■ Without conferring, they should now go and stand in the corner of the room that corresponds to their view.

■ Students take it in turns to argue each other out of their corner. Students should be told that if they hear something very persuasive they should move their position. Students who don't contribute much during verbal debate can also express their views by moving position.

Variations

■ You might want to concentrate on just one statement, thoroughly working through different arguments in the debate.

■ At advanced level you could use 'Debate Around the Room' as a revision activity on a text and work through five or six different contentious statements of the kind that might appear as questions in the exam.

■ Another variation is to ask students to come up with statements for debate themselves. This is a particularly good approach where students are revising a text before an examination.

■ See 'Continuum Opinions' on page 18 for another variation on this activity.

Classroom tips

■ To help the activity along, for example with younger students or with a class that is doing it for the first time, or perhaps where the groups are very unbalanced, you could go and stand in a corner and contribute some arguments. It can also be enjoyable and instructive for students to see the teacher themselves being persuaded to move by a particularly good argument from someone else.

2. Continuum Opinions

AGE	11-18
TIME	15-20 minutes
GROUPING	Whole class
IN BRIEF	**Students respond to statements, for example about an issue, or a character, by placing themselves along a continuum line.**
GOOD FOR	• Highlighting alternative viewpoints.
	• Developing oral argument skills, especially argument-counter argument.
	• Engaging students in thinking about themes and issues before reading and debating questions after reading.
RESOURCES	Controversial or provocative statements about a topic or text.
ON CD ROM	*Studying AQA A Poetry; Much Ado About Nothing – an EMC Study Guide; The Curious Incident – an EMC Study Guide*

Activity

■ Students are asked to envisage an imaginary line between two points in the room, for example, opposite walls labelled 'agree' and 'disagree'. Younger students particularly find it helpful if you create an actual line with a row of chairs or a ribbon.

■ In response to a series of statements, students stand somewhere on the line to indicate how far they agree or disagree with the statement.

■ Ask people to justify their position or try to persuade others to move. Students can move at any time to show that they have changed their mind.

Variations

■ For group work: draw the continuum on a sheet of paper and give students a card with the statement on to move along the line.

■ This activity works well on the interactive whiteboard. Students can come up to the board and move the original statement along the continuum, explaining their decision.

■ The two ends of the continuum do not have to be agree/disagree. For example students could debate where to put a poem on the continuum between any of the following:

poetry/prose; dialect/Standard English; formal/informal; traditional/modern; personal/public; personal/political; subjective/objective; fact/opinion; emotional/unemotional.

■ To discuss appropriate tone for a piece of writing, focus on the title or an exam question with a specific purpose and audience. Place the title on a continuum between 'formal' and 'informal'. Next, look at some sample paragraphs (for example from a previous class's answers to the question). This time students arrange the paragraphs on the same continuum according to their level of formality. Ask them to justify their placing of the paragraphs by referring to vocabulary, punctuation, grammar etc. With some classes you may first need to establish the characteristics of formal and informal writing.

■ See 'Debate Around the Room' on page 17 for another variation.

Classroom tips

■ This activity works best when the statements are provocative or controversial. Encourage students to move about when they are changing their mind, otherwise it can become a bit static.

English Allsorts

3. Inner Circle, Outer Circle

AGE	11-18
TIME	20-60 minutes
GROUPING	Whole class
IN BRIEF	**A small group does a speaking and listening activity in the middle, surrounded by an outer circle of observers.**
GOOD FOR	• Reflecting on the processes of speaking and listening, group work or drama. • Encouraging different levels and kinds of participation. • Allowing sharing of expertise across ability and friendship groups.
RESOURCES	A group of chairs, or space in the middle with an outer circle of chairs for observers.
ON CD ROM	

Activity

- Set up the room in advance and choose a group to do the activity. It could be a group discussion, a role-play or a performance.

- Give the observers in the outer circle a particular focus to make notes for report back in class feedback. The focus could be a particular person, a specific aspect of the text or topic under discussion, or a particular feature of successful group work such as turn-taking.

- At the end of the activity, ask the outer circle for their comments.

- Leave time for each member of the inner circle to respond or comment.

- Try it again with a different group in the inner circle, or give a fresh task to a different group.

Variations

- You could allow the outer circle to interrupt what's happening in the inner circle to comment as the activity is happening. You might want to control the number of interruptions, warning students in advance that you are only going to take a few, so as to avoid losing the momentum of the activity itself.

- You could allow members of the outer circle to take the place of members of the inner circle. This works well in performances or readings, if someone wants to move the interpretation in a different direction.

- You could choose to give each inner circle a sustained chance to complete the task, or you could give everyone a go at being in the middle by making it a quickfire task.

Classroom tips

- If you're reflecting on processes and contributions, set up the ground rules in advance. The feedback from the outer circle should be helpful, not critical, with observers looking for the positive rather than the negative.

- Make sure that students realise that the outer circle roles are just as important as the inner circle roles.

- Build up students' skills with this – don't expect that they'll be expert the very first time they try it.

4. Discussion Rally

AGE	11-18
TIME	20 minutes
GROUPING	Whole class
IN BRIEF	**Structured whole class discussion in which each person builds on the statement of the person before.**
GOOD FOR	• Getting students to develop their ideas in more depth and support their opinions with evidence. • Introducing or reinforcing the argument-counter argument pattern. • Getting everyone involved in a debate.
RESOURCES	A starter statement about an issue or text.
ON CD ROM	Extra Allsort – 2 examples

Activity

■ Make a statement about the issue or text.

■ The first student has five seconds to think and must then say either 'I agree with that because...' or 'I disagree with that because...', giving evidence to support their view.

■ The next student (either a volunteer, the person in the next seat, or a person chosen by the teacher) then comments on that person's statement by saying, 'I agree/ disagree with that because...'

■ The aim is to keep the discussion going as long as possible without 'dropping the ball' (running out of points).

Variations

■ See page 26 for 'Opinion Chains' – a written version of this activity.

■ Another variation is to do the activity physically as a 'relay race', where a group of students get up and stand in line and pass the baton on to each other, trying not to 'drop' it.

Classroom tips

■ Let students know at the beginning of the activity that they are expected to take time to think before contributing – this doesn't have to be a quick-fire discussion. You could make the 5-second thinking time compulsory. Building in the expectation of thinking time means students' responses are more likely to be thoughtful.

■ If the activity is being used to generate ideas for written work, it can be a good idea to appoint a couple of minute takers to record the discussion.

■ You could use the example on the CD ROM as a model to show students how discussion rallies work.

5. The Match

AGE	11-18
TIME	40-50 minutes
GROUPING	Whole class
IN BRIEF	**Using a boxing match format to develop debating skills.**
GOOD FOR	• Highlighting alternative interpretations of a text or issue. • Getting even the shyest students to participate. • Providing stretch and challenge for the most able speakers and listeners.
RESOURCES	A controversial statement; scoring cards. Arrange the room to have a space at the front or in the middle.
ON CD ROM	

Activity

■ Divide the class into an even number of teams, each with four to six members. Pair the groups and give paired groups the same controversial statement – one group to argue in favour, one group against.

■ Establish the ground rules:

● During the match all students can cheer on the competitors but must not call out advice or comments.

● During the match, members of the two teams note points and research evidence ready for the next round. This must be done in silence otherwise they immediately forfeit the match.

■ Each group prepares their arguments and chooses one person to come and present their opening points.

■ The first pair of groups each sends a representative to the front.

■ Sound the start of 'Round 1' and point at the person who should open the debate.

■ Once the debate has begun to get going, the teacher calls the end of 'Round 1'.

■ Participants go back to their 'corners' (i.e. the rest of their group) to get more ideas. The same person can continue to present the arguments, or the group can rotate the role.

■ Call 'Round 2' so that the match begins again.

■ During the debates, the groups who are not part of the current match use a tally mark to keep track of who they think is winning the argument. They could also look out for good argument technique.

■ Keep going for 3-4 rounds or until the groups are beginning to run out of steam. Give a warning before the last round to indicate that this is their last chance to make an impression.

■ Take a class vote as to who has won the 'match', based on their scoring cards.

■ Move on to another pair of groups and let a fresh contest begin.

Classroom tips

■ This activity works best when conducted at a brisk pace. The group representatives need to be fairly confident in speaking and listening.

■ Make your own judgement about whether to have contests for all the groups, or choose between groups. It will depend on how confident the students are, how much they have to say and how much time you have.

6. Popular TV Formats for Talk

AGE	11-18
TIME	40-60 minutes
GROUPING	Small group with whole class performance
IN BRIEF	**Groups use the format of a programme like *The Apprentice* or *Have I Got News for You* to develop speaking and listening, and focus discussion of a set text.**
GOOD FOR	• Providing a structure for talk. • Offering good (and bad!) models of talk for students to follow, or critique. • Pulling together work on a set text and exploring the motivation of characters.
RESOURCES	A short clip from a popular TV programme; a situation or scenario for students to adopt for their own talk.
ON CD ROM	Extra Allsort – 4 suggestions

Activity

■ Show students a short clip from the programme you have chosen.

■ Talk about the format and its conventions. You could also analyse the features of language use at this stage (body language, gestures, turn-taking, agenda-setting and so on), especially if you want to use the activity to think about what makes good group talk.

■ Set up the students either to mimic the tasks set on the programme (for example *The Apprentice*) or do a role-play, in which characters from a set text are involved in a programme, for example:

● A *Big Brother* Diary Room for a character in a set text, followed by their return to talk to the housemates (who could be other characters in the text but need not be).

● Pairs of students come up with a brilliant idea for a product to present to the 'dragons' in *The Dragon's Den* and have to sell their idea to the panel as a Speaking and Listening assessment and/or to teach features of persuasive language.

● Characters from a set text are interviewed on *Desert Island Discs*, giving information about key moments in their lives and choosing music to go with those events.

■ After the task, de-brief it in terms of your key objectives, for example what it revealed about characters in a text, or what it taught students about working in groups.

Variations

■ A media focus: students could create their own brand new format for a TV programme and then do one show in their new format. You could build in extra time for videoing of the students' programmes, to allow for a screening of, and reflection on, each other's work.

Classroom tips

■ You might want to start with an 'analysis' phase, where you look at a clip from a programme and explore the way people talk and listen to each other, before students take up roles themselves.

Reading Any Text

And why not try...

You may also find the following activities useful:

7. A Reading Trail

AGE	11-18
TIME	1 hour to 3 or 4 weeks
GROUPING	Individual, pair and small group with whole class plenaries
IN BRIEF	**An extended activity looking at intertextual links, to encourage thinking about genre, theme, or period, or the way writers work in a tradition and are influenced by each other.**
GOOD FOR	• Encouraging wider reading. • Looking at broader questions about the nature of literature. • Encouraging comparative and cross-curricular thinking.
RESOURCES	A cluster of related texts.
ON CD ROM	*The Curious Incident – an EMC Study Guide; KS3 Poetry Book; The Poetry Pack; Writing from Life*

Activity

■ Provide students with a cluster of texts that are related, so that they can begin to explore generic, thematic or stylistic connections.

The variations below indicate different ways of using this activity.

Variations

■ You might offer groups each of the texts in a different order, to explore what difference that makes. Alternatively, you might look at a core text as a whole class, then share out the other texts between pairs or small groups, so that they introduce their text to the rest of the class and explore connections as a whole class activity.

■ Students could make up their own reading trails. This would be particularly suitable at advanced level for students doing wider reading, perhaps in preparation for synoptic assessment. Their reading trails could form the basis for class work, or timed exam practice for each other.

Classroom tips

■ Make sure you include some interim points when you draw things together as a whole class, as well as at the end.

■ Reading trails can work at different levels, for example supporting contextual study at advanced level or introducing key ideas about poetry or text types at Key Stage 3.

■ Using an interactive whiteboard would be ideal for showing texts across a range of media, such as a painting, or video clip.

■ Creating a visual display to track progress can both motivate students and encourage them to share their reading experiences.

8. Opinion Chains

AGE	11-18
TIME	20 minutes
GROUPING	Individual and whole class
IN BRIEF	**Students share and build on each other's opinions in preparation for writing critically about a text, by adding comments on a piece of paper.**
GOOD FOR	• Helping students to develop their ideas when writing critically about a text. • Drawing attention to different possible interpretations of a text.
RESOURCES	A discussion question
ON CD ROM	Extra Allsort – 4 suggested uses and modelled example

Activity

■ Write a discussion question on the board.

■ Give students a minute to consider their response to the question, in silence without discussion.

■ Students write a few sentences at the top of the paper, summing up their view and backing it up with some evidence.

■ Students pass the paper to the next person. This person writes a comment on the statement. Starter sentences to help students to do this are:

● I agree with this interpretation/comment because...

● I disagree with this interpretation/comment because...

● I find this interpretation/comment interesting because...

● I would like to add...

■ The papers are passed again. This time a student can add their thoughts on either the original statement or any of the subsequent comments.

■ The papers are passed several more times. Three or four of the opinion chains are read out and used to start a class discussion or to help students to plan for an essay.

Classroom tips

■ If you think your students will write rude comments on the papers, either ask them to sign their comment or ask them to pass their comment back to the previous student for checking before passing it on to the next.

Variations

■ This activity would also work well with media texts.

9.   What's on the Agenda?

AGE	14-18
TIME	Variable, 20 minutes to 1 lesson, then ongoing
GROUPING	Individual, pair, small group leading to whole class discussion
IN BRIEF	**Creating an agreed agenda for what's worth considering in a text.**
GOOD FOR	• Making explicit to students the kinds of topics they might need to address in response to a text, or a group of texts.
RESOURCES	None
ON CD ROM	*Studying Othello; Studying Wise Children*

Activity

■ Introduce students to the concept of an agenda – a mental map – for what's worth considering in a text.

■ Ask students to come up with an agenda for writing about narrative in a novel; an agenda for what's specially interesting about the style of a poet; or any other aspect of textual study.

■ Working individually, in pairs or small groups, students list key issues and group them under headings.

■ Collect their ideas on an interactive whiteboard or flipchart and talk through ways of putting them into a coherent set of groupings. Alternatively, show students your own agenda at this stage, adding in anything that the students have thought of that has been missed out.

Variations

■ As students become more familiar with this process, they can write their own agendas for a wide range of different aspects of texts or writing tasks.

Classroom tips

■ This is something that can be set up in a lesson or part of a lesson but is then a continuing element in the study of individual texts, or literary study as a whole. You may want to refer back to elements on the agenda for talking about any poem, play, poem or piece of non-fiction.

■ The idea of an agenda is that students then draw on this list for relevant points to make in answering a question, rather than working through mechanically as a checklist. You're aiming for thoughtful and flexible use of the agenda.

■ An agenda such as this can also be useful for teachers in writing schemes of work, in order to ensure that key issues are covered.

10. How to Ask Good Questions of Texts

AGE	11-18
TIME	Variable, 10 minutes to1 hour
GROUPING	Structured whole class activity, either as a starting-point, or for the whole lesson
IN BRIEF	**Develop thinking skills by helping students to analyse the questions they ask of a text.**
GOOD FOR	• Developing pupils' ability to ask questions of a text and transfer this ability to future texts. • Helping students to weigh up the importance of questions. • Developing close reading and thinking skills on short, complex texts like poems, articles or novel extracts.
RESOURCES	A short text for discussion.
ON CD ROM	*Of Mice and Men – an EMC Study Guide*

Activity

■ Give students a short time to read the text individually and come up with some questions they would like to have answered about it.

■ Pool all of the questions on a flipchart or electronic whiteboard.

■ When no more questions are forthcoming, say that you want five more (the number you ask for depends on how many have already been offered and how much more you think you could expect). Asking for more pushes students to go beyond the obvious and think a bit harder.

■ At this stage, you could take one or both of the following approaches:

● Ask students to categorise and group the questions (questions about the writer's style, the structure, ideas, questions asking for an explanation of something factual and so on)

● Tell the class that they have to reduce the number of questions, leaving only the most important (the number left is up to you, depending on the nature of the text and the number of questions already on the flipchart). Doing this paring down encourages students to think critically about what are key issues, big questions and ones that take you to the heart of the text, as compared with smaller or more peripheral ones. Encourage a debate about the elimination of questions. You could draw on your categorising work, for instance, by suggesting to students that they might want different *kinds* of questions to remain.

■ Students try to answer the questions left on the list, either collectively or in small groups.

■ Finally, having worked through this process, you might ask what kinds of questions provoked the most interesting debate and discussion. Pull out from this activity some things to think about in future work on texts, for example, 'Try asking yourself the kinds of questions that provoke interesting debating points', or 'Try asking yourself questions about form and language as well as ideas'.

■ Students create a list of the kinds of questions one might want to ask of any poem, any piece of non-fiction, any advert, any short story and so on.

Variations

■ Once you've done this with pupils, you could reinforce it by referring back to the discussion when approaching any unseen text. You could also repeat it with new texts, adapting the activity to bring out different aspects of how to ask questions of a text.

■ Another variation might be to work in pairs on two texts, with each pair generating questions on a different text. Pairs swap texts and begin by commenting on each other's questions. They then try to answer each other's questions, before joining up to discuss the two texts. This is ideal for pairing poems and encouraging independent thinking on poetry.

Classroom tips

■ An interactive whiteboard allows you to move questions physically around the board at the categorising and prioritising stage.

■ Give time for thinking – don't rush through!

11. Benchmarking

AGE	11-18
TIME	Variable, 1 lesson to several lessons
GROUPING	Small group work
IN BRIEF	**Students use a scoring grid to compare the features of texts or extracts and make critical judgements about them.**
GOOD FOR	• Scaffolding students in making comparative judgements • Preparing to write a comparative essay.
RESOURCES	Four to five short texts or extracts for comparison; a benchmarking grid (see CD ROM).
ON CD ROM	Extra Allsort – blank grid and comparative statements

Activity

■ Brainstorm (or provide) five criteria for an effective piece of writing of the type you are teaching. For example, if you are comparing short stories, the criteria might be: an intriguing opening, lots of action, evocative description, an interesting main character and a twist in the ending.

■ As a class, read one of the texts and discuss how well it fits the criteria you have agreed. This text is going to be the 'benchmark' text – that is to say it will be the text against which students will compare all the others.

■ In groups or pairs students now read each of the other texts and agree scores in comparison to the benchmark text. Where the comparison text is better than the benchmark, a score of up to +5 can be given. Where the comparison text is worse than the benchmark, a score as low as –5 can be given. For example, if the benchmark short story had a poor opening but the first story for comparison had an opening which really made them want to read on, students might give this story +4 for the opening. However, if the benchmark story had an interesting twist at the end but the story for comparison had an unsurprising ending, students might give this story -3 for the ending.

■ When all the scoring is complete, ask students to total each column: add the + scores together, then add the – scores, and then subtract the minuses from the pluses to get a total score. You could then compare totals across the class to see if the rank orders of the groups are similar or different.

■ After the activity, discuss the criteria: do they work? For example, one of the stories may not have a twist at the end but students may still consider it to have an excellent ending. Do any of the criteria need to be adjusted?

■ Use students' charts as a starting point for modelled and shared writing showing how to make comparisons between the texts. You could give students example sentence starters for comparing texts in that genre. (The CD ROM includes sentence starters for comparing poems.)

■ Students could then go on to write a comparative essay on two or more of the texts, using the chart as a starting point.

Classroom tips

■ The criteria are best when generated by the class, but could be given by you if you are short of time, have a less able class, or want to focus on particular aspects. List the criteria in the first column of the benchmarking grid.

12. Counting Grammatical Constructions

AGE	14-18
TIME	30-60 minutes
GROUPING	Pair or small group, followed by whole class feedback.
IN BRIEF	**A language activity, to encourage close reading of literary or non-literary texts.**
GOOD FOR	• Arousing interest and foregrounding the language features of a text before reading. • Reinforcing language analysis after reading a text. • Teaching about grammar in an embedded context.
RESOURCES	A list of grammatical constructions and/or other language features in an unseen text, such as a poem, speech in a play or newspaper article. This needs to be prepared in advance.
ON CD ROM	*Studying AQA A Poetry*; Extra Allsort – 'Breakfast' by Jacques Prévert; *Studying the World's Wife*

Activity

■ In advance prepare a list of features of the text you've chosen, for example how many dynamic verbs, adjectives, concrete nouns, etc. these are depending on the nature of the text.

■ Allocate one of the features to each pair of students, for example active verbs and passive verbs, first person and second person pronouns, abstract and concrete nouns, prepositions and so on.

■ Without reading the whole text, students count up all the instances they can find of the language feature they have been allocated.

■ Take feed back from each pair and draw up a table of 'statistics'.

■ In pair or whole class discussion, students speculate about what these 'statistics' might show about the nature of the text.

■ Now ask students to read the text and discuss how much they could tell about it just from looking at the list of language features.

Variations

■ 'Counting grammatical constructions' works well during reading as well as for a pre-reading activity. Students read a text and decide what kinds of language features or grammatical constructions it would be interesting to focus on. They conduct the statistical analysis, going on to discuss the insights it gives them into the language of a text.

Classroom tips

■ In preparing the list, you will need to choose which constructions to focus on, according to the text. For instance, it might be useful to count abstract or concrete nouns in a poem by Keats, or count first person pronouns in a poem in Carol Ann Duffy's *The World's Wife*, whereas a different kind of text might throw up other interesting uses of grammar.

13. Becoming a Sub-editor

AGE	11-18
TIME	Variable: 10 minutes to 1 lesson
GROUPING	Individual or pair work, directed from the front and leading to whole class feedback
IN BRIEF	**Use the skills of a sub-editor (writing headlines, standfirsts, sub-heads and pull-quotes) in order to identify the key points in a text.**
GOOD FOR	• Teaching students how to see the 'big picture' when they're reading and sort out the most important points. • Encouraging students to structure their own writing clearly.
RESOURCES	Any text you're studying – particularly good for non-fiction texts such as argument.
ON CD ROM	

Activity

■ Students write a headline for the text, then break it down into sections, giving each section a sub-head.

■ Ask them to write a *standfirst* – one sentence that summarises the key argument or idea being explored in the text.

■ Students now highlight two or three short quotations from the text that are particularly interesting or well-expressed. These are known as *pull-quotes* and are intended to capture the attention of the casual reader.

Variations

■ Depending on the timescale, either do this as a pen and paper activity, annotating the text with ideas for *headings*, *sub-heads* etc. or get students to produce a fully edited version using I.T.

■ Instead of taking a full lesson, this strategy could be a quick 10 minutes used as a way of getting the gist of a text before moving on.

■ Use drama texts and other literary texts, for instance breaking up a key scene into sections or identifying key quotes that give the main gist of the scene.

■ Use sub-editing to develop writing skills:

● Ask students to do the activities listed above on a draft of their own writing. This may uncover problems in the structure of their writing and alert them to places where it isn't clear exactly where their argument is going.

● Alternatively, students write title, standfirst and sub-heads to give them a clear structure for their writing. They then go on to write the essay or article.

■ This could be done as pair work, with students helping each other, or as individual work either in class or for homework. Alternatively, you could model it on an interactive whiteboard as a whole class.

14. Bag of Objects

AGE	11-18
TIME	20-60 minutes
GROUPING	Small group work, whole class performance
IN BRIEF	**Students find in a bag some objects that will orientate them towards a new text.**
GOOD FOR	• Starting a text with a really memorable, fun activity. • Getting students thinking about themes or symbols or moods. • Making students curious about the text they are going to read.
RESOURCES	A collection of objects or images related to the text(s) you are studying, either in a big bag, or placed on tables before students enter the room.
ON CD ROM	*The Curious Incident – an EMC Study Guide;* Extra Allsort – 4 examples

Activity

■ Ask small groups to talk about the objects and improvise a short scene, using the object or objects.

■ Ask students to perform their improvisation and ask observers to take note of key words for each improvisation. Display these words on the classroom walls, so that the class can be reminded of them during the reading of the text.

■ Then read the text. If it is a series of poems, this could follow on from the improvisations quite quickly, to allow students to explore the connections between their improvisations and the texts.

Variations

■ You could either give students the title of the text along with the objects, or choose to withhold this information from them.

■ A quickfire version could be done by asking for volunteers to come up and do an improvisation using the objects, in front of the whole class.

■ You could do this as a carousel, where four or five tables have a different object on them and groups rotate, doing a brief improvisation around each one before moving on to the next table. At each 'change', you could watch a couple of improvisations to see different interpretations.

■ After reading, students could put together a little collection of objects around a text, or moment in a text, so that other students can guess what text or moment is being referred to and why.

■ You could either have one collection of objects for the whole class to look at, or separate collections for different groups.

■ You could use laminated cards in place of actual objects.

Classroom tips

■ This is a lively, potentially noisy activity that needs quite a lot of prior organisation. For a group which enjoys drama activities it's a great way into a text and a highly memorable experience!

15. Circle of Intimacy

AGE	11-18
TIME	40-50 minutes
GROUPING	Individual and pair
IN BRIEF	**A diagrammatic representation of character relationships.**
GOOD FOR	• Thinking about relationships between one character and others in a text. • Exploring character changes through the text.
RESOURCES	None
ON CD ROM	*The Curious Incident – an EMC Study Guide*

Activity

■ To introduce the ideas, students draw a diagram to show the relationships between themselves and the people who are important in their lives. They put themselves in the centre. Triangles represent girls or women and squares represent boys or men. They then place the people who are important to them on the diagram. The closer they are to the centre, the more important they feel the person is to them.

■ Individually or in pairs, students now do a similar diagram for a character in the text and discuss what they notice.

Variations

■ The diagram for a character in the text could be done on the interactive whiteboard, with a class discussion about which characters should be included and where they should be positioned.

■ The diagram could be repeated at different stages to show change, for example the increasing isolation of the Shakespearean tragic hero.

■ This strategy can usefully be applied to media texts such as soaps, sitcoms etc.

Classroom tips

■ For the personal circles of intimacy, make sure that students don't reveal any names. This should avoid students being hurt by where they are placed on each other's diagrams, or having the lesson disrupted by friendship arguments.

16. The Power and the Puddle

AGE	11-18
TIME	20-30 minutes
GROUPING	Whole class
IN BRIEF	**Two students in role negotiate their way around a puddle in the road as a metaphor for power relationships between characters in a text.**
GOOD FOR	• Discussing power relationships in any text. • Discussing different possible interpretations.
RESOURCES	Markers to define the road and the puddle.
ON CD ROM	Extra Allsort – 2 examples; *Sherlock Holmes – an EMC Study Guide*

Activity

■ Explain that at the front of the room there is a pavement. On one side is a busy road, and in the middle of the pavement there is a deep puddle. There is only room for one person at a time to pass by. Set out markers to define the space.

■ Give two students a character each to role play. Do not reveal the character names to the class.

■ The students role play the characters from the text approaching the puddle from different sides and negotiating their way around it.

■ Afterwards the class has to guess the names and status of the two characters from the way they negotiate their way round the puddle and explain their reasoning. At the end of the discussion the 'characters' explain why they behaved as they did.

Variations

■ The character names are revealed to the class in advance. Afterwards the class discuss whether they interpreted the status of the characters in the same way as the actors.

■ Give a pair of students a 'status' card, from a pack of playing cards which you have prepared in advance (2 is lowest, Ace is highest). Ask them each to choose a character they think fits that status and then negotiate their way round the puddle in role. Ask the class to guess who is who and talk about whether they agree about the status level of those characters.

■ Take a named pair of characters and ask different groups of students to mime the same characters at different stages in the play or novel, negotiating their way round the puddle and discussing any changes in the power relationship.

17. Yes And...Yes But

AGE	11-18
TIME	10-40 minutes
GROUPING	Whole class or small groups
IN BRIEF	**Students respond to a text by saying 'Yes and...' and 'Yes but...'**
GOOD FOR	• Thinking actively and critically. • Preparation for argument writing. • Making thoughtful use of literary criticism.
RESOURCES	An argument text, or critical perspective on a literary text.
ON CD ROM	

Activity

■ Students read a text through once.

■ They read it a second time, this time allowing any student to call a halt in order to say either 'Yes and...' or 'Yes but...'.

■ Students could go on to write their views on the text, drawing attention to what they agree or disagree with and explaining why.

Variations

■ This could be done as a paper exercise, where students annotate a text with their 'Yes ands' and 'Yes buts'.

■ You could specify the number of comments you want, for instance at least 3 'Yes ands' and 3 'Yes buts'.

■ This could be done as a 'text-free' activity to develop oral argument skills and argument writing. Give students a contentious statement and then go round the room, with each student either saying 'Yes and' or 'Yes but' to the statement.

18. Soundtrack Storyboards

AGE	11-18
TIME	30 minutes (see variations for longer, more developed uses of this activity)
GROUPING	Pairs or small groups
IN BRIEF	**Choosing a soundtrack to accompany a short extract from a novel, play or poem.**
GOOD FOR	• Providing a context for a close reading of a text. • Highlighting shifts in atmosphere, tension, or tone and focusing students on the way these are created. • Introducing vocabulary for discussing atmosphere, tone and so on.
RESOURCES	Photocopied extract from a novel, play or poem to be annotated, plus a selection of music and sound-effect tracks (five is usually plenty).
ON CD ROM	Extra Allsort – worksheet, text and storyboard grid

Activity

■ In pairs, students read out loud a short extract from their set text/class reader or a poem. They briefly discuss their thoughts about the atmosphere/mood and any shifts they notice and note these on the text.

■ Ask students to think about the type of music or sound-effect tracks they would use to accompany a reading of the extract/poem. At what points do they think there would be a change in the music (or in its volume)?

■ Briefly share first ideas in class discussion, drawing out the reasons for the choices.

■ Play short extracts from the music/sound-effect tracks you have provided, pausing after each one for students to consider whether it might be suitable, at which points in the extract/poem and why.

■ After playing all the tracks give students time to reflect on the ones they would use and the reasons for their choices.

■ Feed back in whole class discussion, supporting students in exploring more fully what it was about the passage which influenced their choices (for example, the content, the language used, the development of the sentences and so on).

Variations

■ Students could research and bring in their own soundtracks.

■ You can make this a shorter, more open activity by asking students to consider the music they would use (for example, upbeat, dying away), rather than providing them with tracks.

■ Students studying a whole text could explore the soundtracks they would use at key points in the novel as a way of recording the changing atmosphere/mood/tone/levels of tension.

■ Rather than creating a soundtrack for an extract from a novel, students could create a soundtrack for a character, using it to trace their changing fortunes, or the way they act in public and in private.

Classroom tips

■ Music composed by Schoenberg, Boulez and Satie works well in this sort of activity, as does ambient music created by Aphex Twin.

19. Opinion Posters

AGE	16-18
TIME	30 mins to 1 hour
GROUPING	Individual, whole class
IN BRIEF	**Students respond in writing to a series of short (provocative) critical readings of their set text, choosing either to challenge or develop the reading and the responses to it.**
GOOD FOR	• Developing argument.
	• Learning how to challenge and develop critical readings.
	• Integrating both critical interpretations and textual evidence into a personal reading of a text.
RESOURCES	A selection of very short extracts from critical readings or reviews, or controversial statements on the set text being studied; large sheets of sugar paper and a thick felt tip pen for each student.
ON CD ROM	*Studying Wise Children*

Activity

- Allocate each student one of the critical readings/controversial statements and ask them to write this in large letters at the top of their sugar paper.

- Students write a short response to the reading/statement, providing one piece of evidence from the text to support their views.

- They pass their paper to the student to the left of them.

- Students read the extract and the response to it. They then add their own comment either extending the first comment or challenging it, with evidence from the text.

- Continue to swap opinion posters until everyone has had the opportunity to add a comment on each critical extract/controversial statement.

- Display the opinion posters on the wall.

Variations

- Students generate the readings/controversial statements themselves.

- Opinion posters can also be used as a way of clarifying and developing arguments for speaking and listening/writing work.

Classroom tips

- The activity works best if the length of the response and the time they have to respond is determined in advance and is kept tight in both cases.

20. Just a Minute Soundbites

AGE	16-18
TIME	30 minutes
GROUPING	Individual, whole class
IN BRIEF	**Students respond orally to 'soundbites' of criticism on their set text.**
GOOD FOR	• Developing argument. • Learning how to respond effectively to critical readings. • Learning how to integrate different readings into a personal response.
RESOURCES	A selection of short 'soundbite' responses to the set text, taken from reviews, longer pieces of criticism and reader responses (from websites such as Amazon).
ON CD ROM	*Studying Spies*

Activity

■ Allocate each student one of the soundbites. They should not share or discuss it with anyone else.

■ Tell students they have two minutes to think about their response and skim the text for evidence to support their interpretation.

■ In turn, students read out their soundbite, followed by a minute's unscripted response, either developing or challenging the reading, with evidence from the text.

Variations

■ After the first student has spoken for one minute, other students could be invited to develop or question either the original soundbite or the 'just a minute' response, perhaps introducing another angle on the reading or adding further evidence from the text which might complicate the reading.

■ Give all students the same soundbite in order to draw out the different responses readers have to texts.

Classroom tips

■ You could use the 'just a minute' responses as the starting-point for a more general discussion. This might focus particularly on the soundbites which provoked a range of responses.

■ Although you may decide to allow students to note down key words as prompts, the activity works best if the 'just a minute' response itself is unscripted.

21. Shifting Tones – Colour Coding a Text

AGE	14-18
TIME	1 hour
GROUPING	Individual, group, whole class plenary
IN BRIEF	**Students colour code a text (poem, extract from a novel) as a way of exploring and visually representing the shifting tones.**
GOOD FOR	• Focusing attention on the detail of a text. • Rooting personal response in the language of the text.
RESOURCES	Photocopies of the text (extract, poem, article) for annotation by each student; a selection of coloured felt-tips.
ON CD ROM	*Studying Wise Children; Studying The World's Wife*

Activity

■ Read the extract or poem, preferably out loud.

■ As a class, brainstorm words to describe its tone, for example bright, moody, angry, fearful and so on.

■ Students read through the list crossing off any words that people find difficult to justify or which are similar to another.

■ Still working as a class, allocate a colour to each tone on the final list.

■ Individually, students read the text using coloured pens to identify the shifts in tone.

■ Students compare 'tonal texts' in small groups, and talk about any striking differences in their choices.

■ Hold a whole class plenary to feed back the main points of the discussion and use these as the starting point of a general discussion on the tone, the way this is created through the language, and its impact on the reader.

Classroom tips

■ Encourage students to do their tonal highlighting privately in the first instance, so that differences of interpretation are revealed in the follow-up discussion.

■ The plenary can be done on the interactive whiteboard so that different groups can show their highlighting.

22. Question Box Revision

AGE	13+
TIME	20 minutes plus 1-2 hours (N.B. This activity works best when completed over two lessons.)
GROUPING	Individual, pair, whole class plenary
IN BRIEF	**Students set their own revision agenda using an anonymous question box.**
GOOD FOR	• Active revision. • Building students' confidence in their knowledge of the topic.
RESOURCES	A small box; slips of paper.
ON CD ROM	

Activity

■ In the first lesson: give each student several slips of paper and allow them around 20 minutes to come up with as many questions as they can on the set text or topic being revised. These can be as complicated or as simple as they wish, but should be genuine questions to which they want answers.

■ In between lessons: check through the questions to weed out any silly ones (but leave in any that seem very basic – the anonymity allows students to ask questions they wouldn't otherwise ask because they know they should know the answer).

■ In the next lesson/s: in pairs, students pick out a question at random from the box. If it is one of their own, they can put it back. Their task is then to research and answer the question. Each pair can do this for as many questions as there is time for.

■ Pairs take it in turns to present their answer to a question to the class. The rest of the class can add any ideas they have in answer to the question, as can the teacher, although the teacher should go last.

Classroom tips

■ With a mixed ability class, you could share out the questions according to ability rather than letting them pick from the box.

■ It is important that students answer the questions on their own, to build confidence, so only help if a pair is very stuck.

23. Visual Representation of a Text

AGE	11-18
TIME	1 hr+
GROUPING	Individual, pair, small group
IN BRIEF	**Representing the structure of a novel, poem or play visually, for example as a diagram, chart, board game or cartoon.**
GOOD FOR	• Exploring the construction and development of a text as a prelude to writing. • Highlighting the connection between 'big' structure (chapters, flashbacks, frame narratives, stanzas) and 'small' structure (motifs, repeated phrases, oppositions and so on).
RESOURCES	Text, large sheets of paper, coloured pens.
ON CD ROM	*Studying Blake's Songs; Studying Othello; The Poetry Pack*

Activity

■ In small groups or as a class, students brainstorm anything they have noticed about the structure of the text, This might be anything from the use of flashbacks, the use of cliffhanger chapter endings, the movement towards a happy ending, the use of a journey or the importance of repeated images.

■ From this extensive list students choose a focus for their visual representation.

■ In pairs or groups, students share ideas about the most effective ways of representing their chosen focus in visual form (for example, a novel tracing the rising and falling fortunes of a character could be represented as a Snakes and Ladders board, while a poem exploring the turning points in an individual's life might be a map).

■ Individually or in pairs, students sketch their visual representation, annotating it to show their thinking.

■ As students present their visual representations, draw attention to the different aspects of the structure highlighted.

■ Use the visual representations as the starting point for a discussion on the connection between the structure of the text, its meaning and the response of the reader.

Classroom tips

■ Emphasise that it is the students' interpretation of the structure and its relationship to its themes and style that is important, not their artistic skills. Rough sketches with annotations work well.

24. Picture Books and Critical Theory

AGE	16-18
TIME	1 hour
GROUPING	Pairs or whole class
IN BRIEF	**Students read a picture book from a range of critical perspectives.**
GOOD FOR	• Introducing critical theory in a fun and accessible way. • Highlighting the insights different critical perspectives can offer. • Encouraging students to engage with, and challenge, critical readings, using textual evidence.
RESOURCES	Enough copies of a picture book for one between two or three students; critical position cards, with simplified summaries of a selection of key literary theories such as feminism, postcolonialism (see CD ROM).
ON CD ROM	*Text, Reader, Critic* – critical position cards

Activity

■ In pairs, students read a children's picture book and share their personal response.

■ Allocate one of the critical position cards to each pair of students and tell them they are now going to re-read the picture book from the perspective summarised on their card.

■ Ask students to talk in pairs about any new insights they have gained into the book through reading from the particular critical position. Does the picture book lose anything from being read from this particular critical perspective? Each pair chooses two or three points from their discussion to feed back in class discussion.

■ Students take it in turns to read out their critical position card and summarise their reading of the picture book.

■ In class discussion, support students in recognising both the different aspects illuminated by the critical positions, and the potential limits of reading only from this perspective.

■ Debrief the activity by talking about how the critical insights gained might be integrated into an independent reading.

Classroom tips

■ Picture books which work particularly well include: *Where the Wild Things Are*; *Burglar Bill*, *Rosie's Walk*; *Not Now Bernard*.

■ Rather than use all the critical position cards with every text, it is often more productive to choose three or four critical positions which you are confident will provoke interesting readings.

■ Use this activity to introduce the critical terms 'foreground' and 'marginalise' – very useful when discussing alternative readings.

■ 'Newsnight Review – a Simulation' (see page 44) supports students in applying critical positions to their set text.

■ You could go on to use 'Opinion Chains' (see page 26) or 'Just a Minute Soundbites' (see page 39) to move students on from considering critical readings discretely to integrating them into a coherent independent reading.

25. Newsnight Review
– a Simulation

AGE	16-18
TIME	1-2 hours
GROUPING	Pairs and group or whole class
IN BRIEF	**Students adopt the role of literary critics on *Newsnight Review* (or similar), discussing their text from the critical perspective they have been allocated.**
GOOD FOR	• Highlighting the insights different critical perspectives can offer.
	• Encouraging students to engage with and challenge critical readings, using textual evidence.
	• Developing students' ability to articulate critical opinions.
RESOURCES	Set text; critical position cards, with simplified summaries of a selection of key literary theories such as feminism, post colonialism (see CD ROM).
ON CD ROM	*Of Mice and Men – an EMC Study Guide; Studying Othello; Text, Reader, Critic*

Activity

■ Allocate a critical position card to each pair of students and tell them they will be discussing the text in role as this critic.

■ Students make notes on which aspects of their set text would most interest a critic reading from this perspective.

■ Each pair prepares a brief introductory statement, highlighting one or two key points about the text.

■ Select a *Newsnight Review* panel, making sure a selection of critical positions is represented. The rest of the class forms the audience, able to contribute to the discussion by request or when invited by the Chair.

■ The 'critics' read out their position statements, before discussing the text more generally, still in role.

■ Debrief the activity by talking about which critical positions seem to be most helpful in illuminating the text.

Variations

■ In order that all students have the opportunity to take on the role of the critic, set up parallel *Newsnight Review* panels. The de-brief can still take place in whole class discussion.

Classroom tips

■ Before tackling this activity, introduce students to critical theory through 'Picture Books and Critical Theory' (page 43).

■ You could go on to use 'Opinion Chains' (see page 26) or 'Just a Minute Soundbites' (see page 39) to move students on from considering critical readings discretely to integrating them into a coherent independent reading.

26. Writing in the Style of

AGE	11-18
TIME	20 minutes to 1 hour
GROUPING	Individual with whole class sharing
IN BRIEF	**Students write the next episode of a narrative in the style of the writer, exaggerating the features they have noticed (e.g. minor sentences, characteristic phrases or lexical choices).**
GOOD FOR	• Alerting students to the key features of a writer's style. • Highlighting the constructed nature of the text.
RESOURCES	Brief outline of an (unread) episode from a novel or scene from a play; the text from which this episode is taken.
ON CD ROM	*Studying AQA A Poetry*

Activity

■ Begin by brainstorming any stylistic features or thematic concerns noticed by the class as characteristic of the writer.

■ Give students a very brief synopsis of the next episode/scene and ask them to write it, drawing on the class list of features and concerns.

■ Students annotate their own writing to show what they were trying to do and how.

■ Listen to the students' episodes, drawing attention to the impact on the reader/listener of the different decisions each made.

■ Finally students compare the choices they made with those of the author, using the exercise as a way of highlighting aspects of style.

Variations

■ Before reading a passage, tell students the basic situation and ask them to write it up in any way they choose, rather than in the style of the writer, making choices about:

● style (e.g. florid, descriptive, spare)

● tense (past, present, a mix?)

● mood (suspense, humour)

● presentation of character

● voice/point of view etc.

■ After listening to, and briefly discussing, the students' work, read the original text. Compare the narrative and linguistic choices made by the author with those made by the students.

Classroom tips

■ Pausing to hear a few fragments of students' writing can be a useful way of showing less able students what is possible.

27. Key Dates – Context

AGE	14-18
TIME	15 minutes
GROUPING	Whole class
IN BRIEF	**Before reading, students use a list of key dates as a quick introduction to thinking about context.**
GOOD FOR	• Starting to think about the context in which a writer lived and worked. • Speculating about how the context might have impacted on the text they are to study.
RESOURCES	A list of key dates and events, chosen for their general importance or particular significance to the writer/text; interactive whiteboard with annotation tools (optional).
ON CD ROM	*Studying Blake's Songs; KS4 Media Pack* – 'Cops on the Box'

Activity

■ Give students copies of the list detailing key dates and events.

■ Read through the list of key dates and events, and ask students to share their first responses.

■ Draw out their responses in class discussion, using the following prompts:

● How would you sum up the period? Can it be captured in a single term? (for example, turbulent, peaceful, prosperous, exciting)?

● What seem to you to be the most significant events?

● Does it seem to have been a stable time or is there evidence of change?

● If you were a writer, what might you have wanted to write about?

■ Return to the dates and the notes both during and after reading, to explore the connection between the key events of the period and the text being studied.

Classroom tips

■ If possible, display the list on the interactive whiteboard.

28. Images and Contexts

AGE	14-18
TIME	30 minutes
GROUPING	Group or whole class
IN BRIEF	**Students explore a selection of paintings and/or photographs as a way of thinking about the social/cultural/historical contexts of a text.**
GOOD FOR	• Getting a sense of the period without having to get a read a great deal. • Starting work on a text in a fun way.
RESOURCES	A selection of images chosen for their connection to the period in which the text was written or is set.
ON CD ROM	*KS3 Fiction Pack; Of Mice and Men – an EMC Study Guide; Studying Sherlock Holmes*

Activity

■ This activity can be adapted for use before, during and after reading.

■ Before reading: provide students with images which give some insight into the period in which the text is set. The example top right is taken from a unit of work on *Othello*. In pairs, students share their impressions of the paintings, focusing on setting, mood, representation of men, women, children and so on. They use their responses to the images to speculate about the text and the themes it might explore.

■ During and after reading: students use post-it notes to annotate the images with quotations from, and references to the text being studied. The example bottom right is taken from a unit of work on *Spies*.

Variations

■ If you have access to PowerPoint, *Picture Power 3* and data projector or interactive whiteboard, with software, this activity is a good whole class starter.

■ Annotating images is also a good way of stimulating creative writing.

29. KWL Grids

AGE	11-16
TIME	Variable
GROUPING	Groups of 3-5
IN BRIEF	**Students set their own agenda to structure research for a fiction or non-fiction text or topic.**
GOOD FOR	• Engaging students by getting them to think about their own research priorities. • Encouraging students to research purposefully. • Discouraging the 'copy and paste' research method.
RESOURCES	
ON CD ROM	*Klondyke Kate Revisited*

Activity

■ Working in groups, students draw up a KWL grid on the chosen topic or text.

● K – what we know

● W – what we want to know

● L – what we've learnt

■ In the 'K' column, students write what they already know on the topic.

■ In the 'W' column the group writes at least one question for each group member.

■ Now group members share out the questions. Each person researches their question and brings the answer back to the group. Answers are collected in the 'L' column ('what we've learnt').

Variations

■ As a revision task, different groups research characters from the text they are studying. The resulting grids can be displayed on the wall.

■ Groups use the KWL grid approach as a way of tackling a challenging poem. In the 'K' column they write what they understand without any teacher intervention. In the 'W' column they write questions they would like

answered. Using dictionaries and each other (still without teacher help) the group work together on the questions and answer as many as they can. Unanswered questions are then shared out for class discussion, with the teacher only intervening if no-one in the class can provide the answers.

■ Before writing an argument piece, the group draws up a KWL grid. Using the Internet, school or local library, students answer their own questions and share the answers. The KWL grid then becomes the starting point for the argument piece.

■ After completing their grids, students evaluate their questions:

● Which were hardest?

● Which were easier to answer?

● Which produced the most interesting answers?

● Which took them deepest into the topic?

30. The Game of the Book

AGE	11-18
TIME	2-3 lessons
GROUPING	Pairs or small groups
IN BRIEF	**Students create a game about the novel or drama text they are studying, for themselves and other students to play.**
GOOD FOR	• Getting a sense of the whole text. • Revising a text and injecting a bit of enthusiasm at a stage when perhaps students are flagging.
RESOURCES	You will probably need to provide card, or cardboard for board games, playing cards and such like. It may be helpful for you to have some small eggtimers, counters and dice, so that students can use these in their games.
ON CD ROM	Extra Allsort – *Spies* game; *Much Ado About Nothing – an EMC Study Guide; Twelfth Night Pack – an EMC Study Guide*

Activity

■ There are 3 phases:

● **Planning the game:**
Pairs or small groups devise the game for small groups to play within the parameters you have set up. For instance, you could make it a requirement that some element of the game involves factual questions, or identifying quotations, or acting in role.

● **Creating the game.**

● **Playing the game.**

Variations

■ Create a game of your own for students to play, or use one that already exists in other publications.

Classroom tips

■ Both the making of the game and the playing of it are useful.

■ You do not need to use class time to complete all these stages. Creating the game could be done, at least in part, for homework. It is important that planning is done in class, so that the maximum value can be extracted in terms of learning about the text.

■ It is helpful to remind students of some game formats that might work well for example *Cranium*, where players have to perform a different kind of task depending where they land, or *Pictionary*, which involves drawing something that's written on a card, or *Trivial Pursuit*, where factual questions have to be answered in order to move on. Simple games like *Snakes and Ladders* could be adapted to have a question and answer element.

31. Zones of Proximity

AGE	14-18
TIME	40 mins to 1 hour
GROUPING	Individual, pair or small group leading to bigger group or whole class plenary
IN BRIEF	**Placing bits of information nearer or further out from the centre of the page, to show how important and useful they are to the topic or text being discussed.**
GOOD FOR	• Evaluating the usefulness of different bits of information to the analysis of a text. • Helping students to prioritise what are the most important ideas.
RESOURCES	10 pieces of contextual information related to the text being studied, cut up and put in an envelope for each group to work with.
ON CD ROM	*Studying Cold Mountain*

Activity

- Students are given 10 bits of contextual information about a text.

- They write the title of their text in the middle of a large sheet of paper or sugar paper.

- They take each bit of information in turn and place it closer to or further from the text/title, depending on how useful they think it is in helping them to interpret the text. If it's completely unhelpful, they don't put it on the paper at all.

- After an agreed period, students compare their zones of proximity diagrams with those of other people and explain why they made the choices they did.

Variations

- This could be done as an interactive whiteboard activity, where the whole class discusses the value of certain bits of information.

- For a more kinaesthetic approach, you could do this as a physical exercise around the classroom, where each student has one piece of information and has to place themselves nearer or further from the centre of the room.

- The same activity can be done in relation to an essay title or exam question with students placing the most interesting and relevant points closest to the title/question.

Classroom tips

- Blutack keeps the contextual cards in place but allows students to re-position them as the activity progresses.

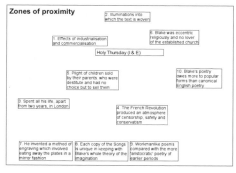

Zones of proximity

2. Illuminations into which the text is woven

6. Blake was eccentric religiously and no lover of the established church

1. Effects of industrialisation and commercialisation

Holy Thursday (I & E)

5. Plight of children sold by their parents, who were destitute and had no choice but to sell them

10. Blake's poetry owes more to popular forms than canonical English poetry

3. Spent all his life, apart from two years, in London

4. The French Revolution produced an atmosphere of censorship, safety and conservatism

7. He invented a method of engraving which involved eating away the plates in a mirror fashion

8. Each copy of the Songs is unique in keeping with Blake's whole theory of the imagination

9. Workmanlike poems compared with the more 'aristocratic' poetry of earlier periods

32. The Text as a Pack of Cards

AGE	11-18
TIME	Variable, depending on options taken
GROUPING	Individual, pair or small group work, with whole class feedback
IN BRIEF	**Students use cards on key aspects of a text as a way of developing interpretation, making connections across the text, preparing for writing or revising.**
GOOD FOR	• Mind-mapping with a kinaesthetic element – moving bits of paper around. • Helping students to think flexibly and make connections. • Reinforcing key elements in a text.
RESOURCES	Key elements of a book (character, themes, images/motifs, narrative techniques) made into sets of cards and laminated for future use.
ON CD ROM	Extra Allsort – *Spies* game; *Studying Wise Children*

Activity

There are at least three possible approaches:

■ Pairs pick a card from the themes pile and a card from the character pile. They have 2 minutes to consider the connections between their two cards, for example what role their character plays in revealing that theme.

■ Pairs or groups look at just one category of cards, for example characters. They cluster their cards in different ways to see patterns and connections between the characters and compare with other groups.

■ Pairs or groups pick one character or theme. They choose from the style, image/motif cards any that seem to relate to the way the writer develops that character and create a mind-map of the writer's techniques to portray the character.

Variations

■ Older or more able students can create their own cards – this pushes them to do the initial thinking about what's important in the text.

■ The cards can be used in revision. For instance, students can pick a card randomly from a hat and be given three minutes to write everything they know about that character, theme, or aspect of style. Or students could be given 60 seconds to speak to the rest of the class about what's on their card. Or they could be asked to write an exam question that's characteristic of their examination specification, using the topic on the card they've pulled out of a hat.

Classroom tips

■ Putting the cards into envelopes at the end will help to keep the sets intact. You could number all of the cards so that you can see very quickly any that have gone missing and replace them if need be.

■ Use different coloured card for each category.

33. Text Transformations

AGE	11-18
TIME	Variable
GROUPING	Individual or pair work
IN BRIEF	**Students adapt a text, turning it into a different genre (in this case a script).**
GOOD FOR	• Developing understanding about genres and their conventions. • Working closely on the detail of a text. • Gaining fresh insight into character and events.
RESOURCES	A photocopy of a short extract from the text being studied.
ON CD ROM	*Three Modern Novels; Great Expectations – an EMC Study Guide; Studying Arthur Miller; Production Practices*

Activity

These instructions are given for transforming a text into a script.

■ Ask students to decide how to adapt the text extract, as a drama script, TV or film script. Students use highlighter pens to select dialogue, then annotate the text with ideas about how to convey action, behaviour or settings through stage directions.

■ Students write the scripts, adding extra dialogue where necessary to convey something which, in the original, is told through the narrative voice.

■ They perform the adaptations to the class

■ Students compare their scripts with the original text and are encouraged to consider:

● how well different adaptations brought out aspects of the original

● what the activity has revealed about the strengths of prose narratives

● what the activity has revealed about the strengths of a script

● what new insights they have gained into the original, for instance characters whose motivation they understand more fully, or a different slant on an important event.

Variations

■ Provide students with the script of an adaptation of a key moment in a prose text. Ask them to compare the script with the original, in order to explore what can be learned about the original text.

■ Text transformations can be done with a range of different genres:

● novel to poem

● poem to prose narrative

● play extract to prose narrative

● non-fiction text to prose narrative

● prose narrative to non-fiction text

● novel to musical theatre.

■ For a lengthier project, you could video the adaptations as short TV/film dramas.

Classroom tips

■ Try to keep the focus on the original text and what the transformation can reveal about that. Where students start to veer off at a tangent, bring them back to the essence of the activity. On the other hand, allow experimentation that might get to the mood, or deeper levels of analysis of character in unusual or expressionist ways.

34. Turning a Text into a Recipe

AGE	11-18
TIME	45 mins to 1 hour
GROUPING	Individual or pair work
IN BRIEF	**A writing task on a class reader or set text, with a fun element.**
GOOD FOR	• Summarising a text for revision or pulling together ideas in a creative way.
	• Thinking about the 'ingredients' that go into a text, so emphasising the role of the writer in pulling together lots of different elements and making choices.
RESOURCES	Class reader or set text
ON CD ROM	

Activity

■ Ask students to write the text they've been studying as a recipe, with a list of ingredients and a set of instructions, to show how the writer has concocted the story, for instance:

- the ingredients (characters, themes, styles of writing)

- quantities (a pinch, a dash, several pints, lashings of...) to show what's important

- instructions/method (the writer's techniques)

■ Read some of the recipes aloud, to share what students have written.

■ Ask students to write a short commentary, explaining their recipe and how it relates to the original text.

Variations

■ Try other unusual short genres, as a fun way of summarising a text. For instance, an advert, a spell, an encyclopaedia entry, a rap, a set of directions.

■ This strategy also works well as a way of coming up with success criteria for a piece of writing.

Classroom tips

■ Read out little bits of students' writing along the way, to give other students ideas about what to do and share the fun!

35. Role-Play Prediction

AGE	11-18
TIME	40-50 minutes
GROUPING	Small group and whole class
IN BRIEF	**Students role play the next, unread scene in a play or episode in a novel, to speculate about what might happen.**
GOOD FOR	• Considering the plot choices writers make.
	• Pulling together what students know so far in their reading of a text and considering how the characters might behave.
	• Exploring what students know about the way plots develop.
RESOURCES	Role cards for each of the characters in the unread scene or episode, with prompts about the situation the character will be in and some points to consider about how the character might react.
ON CD ROM	*Great Expectations – an EMC Study Guide; Much Ado About Nothing – an EMC Study Guide*

Activity

■ Put the students into groups, matching the number of characters in the scene or episode.

■ Give each student a character role card and give them a bit of time individually to sort out their ideas about the situation, their likely role and reactions.

■ Ask the groups to improvise the scene once.

■ Now ask them to rehearse it again, developing more fully their ideas about the scene.

■ Let the whole class watch two or three of the scenes and talk about different interpretations of characters and different choices a dramatist might make.

■ Finally, as a whole class, read aloud the scene as originally written and compare it with the choices made by the different groups.

Classroom tips

■ This will only work if students genuinely don't know what's going to happen next. It's no good if they've already seen a film adaptation, for instance.

■ It is best if group sizes are limited to 2-3 and students are given only one aspect or situation from the next scene or chapter to role play.

■ When using improvisations it can be useful to ask students to begin and end the scene with a freeze-frame. This avoids never-ending scenes, or ones that just tail off.

Poetry

And why not try...

You may also find the following activities useful:

36. Collapsed Poem

AGE	11-18
TIME	Pair
GROUPING	20 minutes
IN BRIEF	**Students study an alphabetical list of words from a poem, speech, or short, linguistically interesting passage from a novel.**
GOOD FOR	• Focusing attention on the language of the text, both out of context and then in the context of the original text.
RESOURCES	A 'collapsed' text, with all the words sorted and arranged alphabetically; the original text.
ON CD ROM	*Studying AQA A Poetry; Studying Blake's Songs; Richard III – an EMC Study Guide*

Activity

■ In pairs, students explore the collapsed text, noticing repetitions, patterns, oppositions, word groups.

■ Feed back observations.

■ In class discussion begin to speculate about the type of text this might be.

■ Read the text, using the analysis of the decontextualised words as a way into thinking about their use and impact within the text.

Variations

■ Ask students to speculate about the title of the poem before investigating the collapsed text.

■ You could vary the activity by leaving the punctuation in the collapsed version so that students know which words end a sentence or begin a line/sentence.

■ After analysing the collapsed text, students could go on to use the words to create their own text, along the lines of 'Using a Poet's Words' (see page 64).

How to collapse any text

1. Make sure the original text is saved.

2. Highlight the text and keep it highlighted throughout.

3. Go to the Edit menu.

4. Choose 'Replace'.

5. Type a space in the top box.

6. Type a ^p in the lower box.

7. Choose 'Replace all'.

8. Choose 'No'.

9. Choose 'Close'.

10. Choose 'Table'.

11. Choose 'Sort AZ', (or on an Apple, choose 'Sort' and 'Sort by Field 1')

12. Choose 'OK'.

37. Desert Island Poems

AGE	11-18
TIME	1 hour+
GROUPING	Individual, pair or small group work, followed by whole class presentation.
IN BRIEF	**Students are let loose on a range of poetry anthologies and are asked to create their selection for 'Desert Island Poems'.**
GOOD FOR	• Encouraging reading poetry for pleasure. • Encouraging broader skills with books such as skimming, scanning, using contents and index pages. • Developing skills of presentation and reading aloud.
RESOURCES	A wide range of poetry anthologies.
ON CD ROM	*KS3 Poetry Book* – variation on choosing a sonnet for a radio programme

Activity

■ Provide students with a wide range of anthologies and tell them they have been invited to select their favourite poems for a new radio show based on the long-running programme *Desert Island Discs*.

■ After a set period of time, ask students to present their choices. This can be done as a straight poetry reading, with a short introduction explaining the choice of each poem, or it can be done more like *Desert Island Discs* itself, with an interviewer asking the student questions about the choice of poems, before each one is read aloud by another member of the group.

Variations

■ You could do the same activity with other literary forms, although poems are particularly good because they are short enough to read aloud and the 'trawling' process can be undertaken in however much time is available.

■ Pairs or groups of students can also be asked to choose their 'Desert Island Poems'. For this variation provide a set of criteria to consider when drawing up a longlist for discussion and voting, for instance:

● Do you want to make sure that there's some variety, in terms of mood, theme, period, gender or will all your poems be of one kind?

● Length?

● Will you choose poems that say something special to you, or will you go for famous ones?

● Are they poems that will bear listening to/reading over and over again?

■ Students could do this in role, as a celebrity or other person they know a lot about.

■ Although ideally suited to 11-14-year-olds, this is also an activity you could use to inject a bit more energy and enthusiasm for poetry at 14-16-year-olds and advanced level, perhaps a one-off lesson early in the course or on National Poetry Day.

Classroom tips

■ The number of poems to be selected can be changed to suit the time available and size of groups, for instance just three poems for a single lesson activity. If the activity is more extended, or if individuals are selecting poems, they could be asked to choose eight or 10.

38. Getting the Rhythm

AGE	11-18
TIME	30-45 minutes
GROUPING	Individual or pair
IN BRIEF	**A structured approach to teaching about rhythm.**
GOOD FOR	• Giving students the confidence to talk and write about rhythm, without getting too hung up on technical terms.
RESOURCES	A list of words for rhythms, such as lilting, pounding, sing-song, jumpy etc and a poem or group of poems.
ON CD ROM	*Studying Blake's Songs;* Extra Allsort – *emagazine* guide to rhythm

Activity

■ Start by reading the poem or poems aloud, to get an initial feel for the rhythms.

■ Get students up on their feet, wandering around the room, each reading aloud and walking, moving, swaying or dancing as they speak the words. They could all be reading the same poem or different ones. Be prepared for a cacophony of noise!

■ Give students a sheet with a list of words that could be used to describe rhythms or try getting them to brainstorm a list of words themselves.

■ Ask them to think about which words best apply to the rhythm of the poem they have been reading. Share views as a whole class.

■ Ask students to complete starter sentences, such as the ones on the CD ROM, using examples from the poems they are studying.

■ Read out some of the completed sentences. Talk about how appropriate the choice of rhythm words was for the poems used as examples.

■ Work together on the sentences to strengthen them, particularly in terms of modelling the way in which the effects of rhythmic patterns can be analysed.

Variations

■ Students could walk round the room, clicking their fingers to the beat, or stamping their feet, to emphasise the pattern of beats to the line.

■ Have a collection of anthologies available, in a book box. Give students an adjective describing a rhythm. Ask them to skim through an anthology, looking for a short extract from a poem that seems to them to have that rhythm, for example 'Look for a poem with a broken, jumpy rhythm'.

Classroom tips

■ Do plenty of reading aloud and experimenting with different ways of reading to get a first 'feel' for the rhythms. Then move into capturing this in words.

39. Poem Shapes

AGE	11-18
TIME	15-30 minutes
GROUPING	Whole class, pairs or small groups
IN BRIEF	**A quick activity to introduce ideas about the look of poems on the page, their form and structure.**
GOOD FOR	• Getting students to think about the importance of the 'look' of a poem, its length, structure and form without the distraction of searching for meaning.
RESOURCES	Blacked-out versions of the poems plus the poems themselves. (See 'Classroom tips' below)
ON CD ROM	*Studying AQA A Poetry; KS3 Poetry Book; Texts in their Times – Victorian and Modern*

Activity

■ Show two or three poem shapes to students and ask them to think about any ideas they may have about the poem(s) by just looking at their shapes. They might consider similarities and differences.

■ Now ask students to read the poems to see how far their judgements are borne out by the poems themselves.

Variations

■ You could explore the impact of shape on a single poem before studying it, as opposed to doing a comparative activity.

■ An interactive whiteboard allows you to erase sections of highlighting to test out students' predictions, for example whether an indented line at the end of each stanza means there is use of repetition.

■ 'Poem Shapes' can also be used after reading as a focus for exploring issues of form and structure.

Classroom tips

■ This activity is ideal for 14-16-year-olds and advanced level study, where a close focus on form and structure is important, but equally can work well at 11-14-year-olds, to look at haikus, riddles, sonnets and other specific forms.

■ Choose poems with quite different forms (for example one short lyric in regular quatrains and one longer poem in free verse, with long lines of irregular length). Cover the entire text in black, following the shape of the poems, in Word or on paper. This can be done using black felt tip and turning the sheets into OHTs.

■ Prepare the text as a Word document or in your interactive whiteboard software, using the 'highlight' facility to black out the text. This would allow you to show the poem shapes on an interactive whiteboard.

40. Reading a Poem Line-by-Line

AGE	11-18
TIME	20- 60 minutes
GROUPING	Whole class
IN BRIEF	**Exploring poetry by revealing a poem bit by bit.**
GOOD FOR	• Encouraging exploratory thinking, rather than a narrowing down of meanings. • Developing close reading strategies. • Focusing on language, looking at patterns as well as meaning.
RESOURCES	OHP or interactive whiteboard, with poem pre-prepared. The poem should be one that students have not seen before.
ON CD ROM	*Studying Blake's Songs;* Extra Allsorts – Billy Collins''Introduction to Poetry'and Charles Causley's 'I am the Song'

Activity

■ Put a copy of a poem up on the screen, revealing only a line or part of a line at a time.

■ Each time you stop, ask students to make predictions and then revise them in the light of new evidence. As each new line is revealed, discuss the implications of individual words and their impact.

■ Choose whether or not to reveal the title at the beginning or the end, depending on the poem. You can ask students to suggest titles of their own before revealing the actual title.

Variations

■ Look just at the opening line and the last line before reading the whole poem.

■ Look just at the title and opening line, as a prediction exercise before reading the whole poem.

■ Look just at the opening or closing lines of stanzas before reading the whole poem.

■ Reveal the poem word-by-word or phrase by phrase.

■ Reveal between five and 10 random words, followed by another group of random words to begin to guess at what you can tell about the poem, before reading the whole text.

Classroom tips

■ The choice of poem is important. Try revealing the poem to yourself bit by bit to see how it works. A few examples of poems that work particularly well are:

– 'The Gift' – Carol Rumens

– 'The Clod and the Pebble' – Blake

– 'Ode on Melancholy' – Keats

– 'Introduction to Poetry' – Billy Collins

– 'I am the Song' – Charles Causley

■ There are several ways of revealing the poem line by line: in interactive whiteboard programs use the 'rollerblind' or 'screenshade' tool; in Word highlight the whole text in black before the start of the lesson and then 'un-highlight' the text to reveal it bit by bit.

41. Sound Patterns

AGE	11-18
TIME	40-50 minutes
GROUPING	Pairs or small groups
IN BRIEF	**Students work with a cut up version of a poem in which sounds are important, before reading the poem itself.**
GOOD FOR	• Looking closely at patterns and connections in the way the poet has used sounds in a poem. • Looking at how the sounds relate to meaning.
RESOURCES	A poem cut up line-by-line, with each line numbered for ease of reference.
ON CD ROM	Extra Allsort – classroom material and teachers' notes on 'The Clod and the Pebble'; *Studying The World's Wife*

Activity

■ Ask pairs or small groups to look at the cut-up lines from a poem, at this stage without worrying about the meanings of the lines.

■ Remind students that they are looking at the words within a line as well as the words that end a line.

■ Ask students to group the lines in any way they like according to the sounds only, rather than meaning. (This might include hard/soft sounds, use of rhyme, use of alliteration, assonance, onomatopoeia but should be left to students to decide.)

■ Each time they create a grouping they make a note of what links the lines for instance, lines 1, 5 and 6 all rhyme or lines 1, 2 and 3 all include lots of words with 'p' sounds.

■ Now give students the whole poem to read. This time they discuss the meaning of the poem and look at how their sound groupings relate to the meaning.

■ Groups feed back to the rest of the class. Sentence starters can help, such as:

● When we grouped the lines according to rhyme, we noticed that ...

● When we grouped the lines according to alliteration, we noticed that ...

Classroom tips

■ You may want to revise some of the ways poets might use sounds in a poem before starting the activity, if you feel that this is necessary.

42. Pair-Split-Pair

AGE	11-18
TIME	60 minutes
GROUPING	Pair with whole class plenary
IN BRIEF	**Students work with several different partners on a challenging poem.**
GOOD FOR	• Building students' confidence in their ability to tackle a challenging poem. • Highlighting different ways of reading a poem.
RESOURCES	A challenging poem, one copy per pair.
ON CD ROM	

Activity

■ Read the poem aloud to the class.

■ In pairs, students re-read the poem. Give them around 10 minutes to come up with one statement they think is true about the poem and one question they would like answered.

■ Students call themselves 'A' or 'B' in their pair. Bs stand and move to a new partner, leaving the poem and notes with A.

■ In the new pair, B reads A's statement and discuss whether they agree or disagree on these. Together they then try to answer A's question and note any possible answers. If they resolve the question to each other's satisfaction, they then think of a new question they would like answered. Allow around 15 minutes for this stage.

■ Repeat the last two steps at least once more. If you have time, repeat three more times.

■ Hold a whole class plenary, discussing what students can now say about the poem and discussing any unanswered questions.

Variations

■ Although particularly suitable for poetry, this strategy can be used with any short text, including non-literary ones.

Classroom tips

■ The point of the activity is for students to work independently to build confidence, so only help if a pair is very stuck.

■ Poems which work well include (in order of difficulty): 'The Stare' by Sujata Bhatt, 'Hawk Roosting' by Ted Hughes, and 'Windhover' by Gerrard Manley Hopkins.

43. Using a Poet's Words

AGE	11-18
TIME	Individual
GROUPING	10-20 minutes
IN BRIEF	**Students use the words from a poem they are going to study to write their own.**
GOOD FOR	• Making students familiar with the language of a poem. • Whetting students' appetites for reading a poem. • Encouraging students to write poetry alongside the reading of it.
RESOURCES	A poem, presented first as a list of words and then in its original published form.
ON CD ROM	*Studying Blake's Songs;* Extra Allsort – classroom material on 'Tichborne's Elegy'

Activity

- Give students a list of all the words taken from the poem they are going to study.

- Tell them to use the words in any way they want to create a poem.

- Listen to a selection of the poems and, as a class, talk about the similarities and differences in both content (ideas, themes, arguments) and style (techniques).

- Read the original poem. Use the students' poems and their similarities with/differences from the published poem as a way into exploring their response to this text.

Variations

- You can differentiate the activity by insisting that students use all the words from the poem and no more, or by allowing them to miss out a limited number, or allowing them to add a number of their own words.

Classroom tips

- This activity works well as a quick whole class activity on an interactive whiteboard. As students make suggestions they can be asked to articulate the thinking behind their ideas, thus drawing attention to the creative writing process. It can also form a useful context for modelling effective re-drafting.

44. Spot the Poet

AGE	14-18
TIME	40+ minutes
GROUPING	Pair or group work
IN BRIEF	**A game, where students see if they can spot which poem is by the poet they are studying.**
GOOD FOR	• Revising the work of a poet and clarifying his/her key features.
RESOURCES	Four or five poems by different poets, including one or two by the poet whose work students are studying but which they have not seen before.
ON CD ROM	

Activity

- Ask students to decide which poems are by their set poet and justify their views with evidence from the poems.

- Follow up the group work with a whole class plenary weighing up the evidence. Use the plenary to create a list of 'key features' of the poet's work.

Variations

- As an advanced level homework task students can write their own stanzas, as if they are long lost fragments by the set poet (not to be seen by anyone else and submitted in typewritten form). You can then mix in these stanzas with stanzas from poems by the set poet that haven't been studied in class. Students then guess which are real, which fake. If you do it as a game, you can award one point to each student who makes a correct guess and one point to each student whose 'faked' stanza is identified as being by the set poet.

- A more challenging activity for strong advanced level classes is to choose poems by other poets where some features overlap with those of the studied poet but where there are also subtle differences.

Classroom tips

- The poem by the set poet should be one that they have not come across before but should be fairly typical of themes and/or style. The poems by the other poets should be recognisably different in terms of style or theme (although see Variations for a more challenging advanced level option).

- Let students know that this activity is less about 'getting it right' and more about justifying a viewpoint with evidence from the poems. The discussion is as important as the final decisions.

- Use the list of 'key features' drawn up during the plenary as a revision tool.

Prose Fiction

45. The Digested Read

AGE	14-18
TIME	1 hour
GROUPING	Individual or small groups, with whole class plenary
IN BRIEF	**Write a 400-word version of a set text parodying or exaggerating the style of the original.**
GOOD FOR	• Highlighting the key aspects of the novel. • Highlighting its stylistic features. • Drawing attention to different readings.
RESOURCES	Copies of the set text being studied and examples of the *Guardian's* 'digested reads' (see 'The Digested Read' archive at http://books.guardian.co.uk/).
ON CD ROM	Extra Allsort – John Crace's digested read of *Harry Potter and the Deathly Hallows*

Activity

■ Introduce the concept of the 'digested read' and show students a few examples from the *Guardian* website.

■ Students make notes on what they would include in a digested read of their set text and share these first ideas in small groups or as a class.

■ In groups, draw up a list of stylistic features characteristic of the set text, for example frequent use of metaphor or short incomplete sentences.

■ Feed back the stylistic features in whole class discussion, suggesting how the style of the digested read might reflect the style of the original.

■ Individually, students draft their 400-word digested set text.

■ In groups or as a class, students take it in turns to read aloud their digested reads.

■ Talk about what each person has foregrounded (given a lot of space to) or marginalised (pushed into the background or given very little space to) in terms of content and style.

■ Talk about the similarities and differences in the interpretations of the set text.

Variations

■ The *Guardian* also includes a single sentence of the text – 'the digested read, digested'. Having written a digested read, students can attempt to condense their interpretation of the novel into a single sentence or try to summarise the novel as a standard length text message (160 characters).

Variations

■ Media texts can be usefully digested in this way (see 'Instant Synopses' on page 142).

Classroom tips

■ See http://books.guardian.co.uk/ for a wide selection of John Crace's 'digested reads', both contemporary fiction and non-fiction (including lighter 'celebrity' autobiographies).

46. Headlining a Novel

AGE	13-18
TIME	1 lesson
GROUPING	Individual or pair with whole class feedback
IN BRIEF	**Students sum up a chapter or novel in a series of headlines.**
GOOD FOR	• Highlighting structure. • Drawing attention to different readings of a text. • Creating a personal summary of the text, helping students get a handle on the text.
RESOURCES	Set text
ON CD ROM	

Activity

- As a class, divide the chapter or novel into sections.

- If the whole novel is the focus of the activity, allocate chapters to different pairs.

- In pairs, students re-read the chapter or section they have been allocated, summing up its main focus in between eight and 12 headlines.

- Take it in turns to read out the headlines in sequence.

- Talk about the similarities and differences in what students chose to focus on (or foreground).

- Use the headlines as the starting point for exploring the structure of the chapter/section in more detail.

Variations

- Rather than headlines, students can sum up each section in no more than three words, or a single sentence, or select a single quotation. The latter is particularly useful for students preparing for a closed text exam.

- This activity also works well for poetry, particularly narrative poetry; Coleridge's glosses to *The Ancient Mariner* provide a good model.

Classroom tips

- If you want to end up with a summary of the whole novel, allocate single chapters to different students. It's worth getting more than one student to work on each chapter so that students see which aspects of the text different students have chosen to emphasise.

47. Open the Book

AGE	13-18
TIME	20-60 minutes
GROUPING	Individual or pair work, leading to whole class discussion.
IN BRIEF	**Students randomly open the novel they are studying and use the evidence they find to discover more about the writer's prose style.**
GOOD FOR	• Analysing narrative prose style, in an enjoyable and unusual way.
RESOURCES	Class novel/set text.
ON CD ROM	Extra Allsort – suggestions for a single novel and comparative study

Activity

- Ask students to open the novel at a random page.

- Give them a list of things to count, or estimate. For instance, ask them to do the following:

  - Estimate the percentage of dialogue on the page.

  - Count the number of polysyllabic words in the first 100 words.

  - Look at the first 10 sentences. Count the number of simple sentences, compound sentences, complex sentences and minor sentences (for example 'Drat!' or 'At last.').

  - Look at the first 10 sentences. Count the number of questions, statements, commands and exclamations.

- Ask students to compare their findings with another group, or as a whole class.

- Together, discuss what, if anything, these findings seem to reveal about the characteristics of the novelist's prose style.

Variations

- Depending on the text, you might want to look at two or three different moments in the same text to make a comparison of the writer's style and techniques used.

- You could extend the activity to create mathematical graphs or charts to show the balance of different kinds of narration or types of sentences in the text. You might even want to compare two writers by plotting the same features on a graph to show differences of style.

Classroom tips

- Vary the number of things you choose to focus on, depending on the age and stage that students are at and their confidence with language terms and concepts.

48. Story Shape Diagrams

AGE	11-18
TIME	1-2 hours
GROUPING	Individual, pair or group work
IN BRIEF	**Students look at diagrammatic representations of narratives, or create their own.**
GOOD FOR	• Getting a sense of the whole structure of a novel. • Thinking about different narrative structures. • Creating narratives of their own.
RESOURCES	A few sketches of diagram shapes to act as examples.
ON CD ROM	*Great Expectations – an EMC Study Guide; KS2 English and Literacy Pack; Writing from Life*

Activity

■ Show students three or four different kinds of diagrams that might represent the story or novel that they have been studying. Ask them to pick the one that best seems to represent their story and give reasons for their decision.

■ Ask them to plot in detail key moments in the story on their diagram.

Variations

■ Offer students a story shape as a way of planning a story of their own. For instance, they could work out a brief storyline chronologically: this happens, then this happens and so on. They could then decide where they are going to put these events onto their story shape. For instance, the story might start somewhere in the middle of the chronological events, or even at the end.

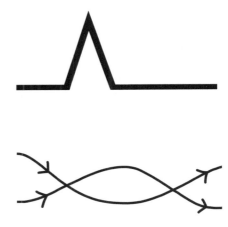

Drama

And why not try...

You may also find the following activities useful:

Speaking and Listening:

Media Simulations:

49. Cast Meeting

AGE	11-18
TIME	40-50 minutes
GROUPING	Whole class and group work
IN BRIEF	**After reading a scene from a drama text, students in role as actors and director simulate a cast meeting to discuss different ways of playing the scene.**
GOOD FOR	• Discussing different possible interpretations. • Discussing how a scene contributes to plot and character development.
RESOURCES	A scene from the drama text being studied.
ON CD ROM	Extra Allsort – *Richard III* example; *Pre-1770 Drama – Elizabethan and Jacobean*

Activity

■ As a class, discuss which aspects of the scene are open to being performed in a number of different ways. Talk about some of the possible ways of playing and directing it.

■ Put students into 'sharing' groups of at least four people. Each student should be allocated the role of either an actor playing one of the characters in the scene or the director.

■ Before any discussion, students form a new 'expert' group with at least three others considering the scene from the same point of view (in other words, groups of 'actors' playing the same character or groups of 'directors').

■ Give students a limited time to prepare for a cast meeting in which they will discuss the pros and cons of different ways of playing the scene and decide on their preferred option.

■ Still in role, the actors should consider how they see their character in the rest of the play and what would be the most interesting way to play the scene from an actor's point of view. They should find some quotations and examples to support their opinions about the character.

■ The students in role as the director should consider what would have the best dramatic effect and how they want the audience to think and feel at this point in the play. They should also find some quotations and examples to support their opinions.

■ Students return to their 'sharing' group (so that each group has at least one person who has considered each point of view). They now hold the 'cast meeting', discussing in role the best way to play the scene. In addition to contributing their view of how the scene should be played, the pupil in role as director should chair the meeting.

■ Groups can go on to compare their decisions with those of other groups.

Classroom tips

■ This activity works best when students focus on the actions of two or three characters.

■ Keep preparation for the cast meeting short, perhaps 15 minutes.

50. Cheering and Groaning Summary

AGE	11-14
TIME	30 minutes
GROUPING	Whole class
IN BRIEF	**As a before reading activity, students listen to a summary of the play, cheering every time 'their' character's fortunes rise and groaning every time they fall.**
GOOD FOR	• Actively familiarising students with plot, characters and relationships before reading. • Highlighting the changing fortunes of characters and alerting students to key themes and structural features.
RESOURCES	A summary of the text to be studied, broken down into simple statements; cards with character names on them.
ON CD ROM	Extra Allsort – classroom material on *Much Ado About Nothing; Richard III – an EMC Study Guide*

Activity

■ Allocate key characters to each pair of students, along with the statement-by-statement summary of the play.

■ Students read the summary, marking each statement according to whether their fortunes seem to be rising, falling or remaining steady.

■ Read the summary out loud, pausing after each statement to allow students time to cheer or groan and wave their cards in the air.

Variation

■ The 'Cheering and Groaning Summary' is a useful revision activity. If used in this way, students could go on to chart the rising and falling fortunes of their character, choosing short quotations as evidence of their interpretation.

Classroom tips

■ Limit the number of characters, choosing only those who play a substantial part in the play.

51. Conversation Analysis

AGE	11-18
TIME	20-60 minutes
GROUPING	Pairs, small groups or whole class
IN BRIEF	**When reading drama texts, apply the concepts that linguists use to analyse spontaneous speech.**
GOOD FOR	• Revealing power relationships in drama. • Looking at ways in which dramatists capture the qualities of real spoken exchanges.
RESOURCES	Extract
ON CD ROM	*Studying Othello; Richard III – an EMC Study Guide*

Activity

■ Give students some of the basic concepts of conversation analysis:

- turn-taking and how this can show power, rudeness or politeness

- agenda-setting and how this can show power relationships, assertiveness etc.

- interruptions and what they reveal

- length of utterances and what they reveal

- kinds of sentences (statements, commands, exclamations and questions) and what they reveal about power relationships, conflict, politeness and so on

- adjacency pairs – conventional patterns in conversation, such as greeting/greeting or question/answer and what happens when the patterns are flouted.

■ Ask students to analyse a short segment of a drama text using these ideas about the way conversation works.

■ Discuss what the analysis reveals about the relationships between the characters and the techniques used by the dramatist.

Classroom tips

■ This can be done at different levels with different age groups. At 11-14-years you might want to focus on just a few aspects of conversation analysis that seem particularly important in the scene you're looking at, rather than expecting a thorough-going analysis of all aspects. They would not need all the terminology to do the activity.

■ One way of developing students' independence in using these ideas is to give pairs of students one aspect of conversation analysis to focus on and report back on to the rest of the class.

Variation

■ This strategy also works well when studying TV or film drama extracts, for example *Holby City*, sitcoms etc.

52. Looking at the Cast List

AGE	11-18
TIME	20-30 minutes
GROUPING	Individual, small group or whole class
IN BRIEF	**Making predictions from the cast list as a pre-reading activity.**
GOOD FOR	• Helping students to engage with elements of the text before starting to read. • Drawing attention to possible relationships between characters. • Enabling students to speculate and make predictions about genre, plot and so on.
RESOURCES	Cast list
ON CD ROM	*Much Ado About Nothing – an EMC Study Guide; Studying Wise Children*

Activity

■ Show students the cast list of the play as it appears in the text.

■ Students speculate and predict as much as they can about the play, for example possible themes or relationships between characters, using prompts such as the ones below:

● What immediately strikes you about the characters and the way they are described?

● How is the character list organised?

● What type of play do you think this is?

● What do you think the story of the play might be?

● What themes do you think might be explored?

Variations

■ This strategy can be be usefully applied to TV drama, with students looking closely at the presentation of the cast lists in TV listings magazines such as the *Radio Times*.

■ Students write their own 50-100 word synopsis of a possible drama using those characters. They share synopses before starting to read the play.

Classroom tips

■ Encourage students to go beyond predicting plot to think about the drama, for example a very large cast might imply a different kind of drama to one with just three or four characters.

53. The Panto Audience

AGE	11-18
TIME	20-30 minutes
GROUPING	Small group and whole class
IN BRIEF	**Getting the class involved as a kind of chorus when a group perform a scene.**
GOOD FOR	• Highlighting possible audience responses to elements such as: dramatic irony; relationships between characters; what the audience already know; predicting what might happen next.
RESOURCES	Scene from a set text.
ON CD ROM	*Much Ado About Nothing – an EMC Study Guide*

Activity

- In groups, students read the scene, briefly discussing the advice or instructions they might give a character at different stages.

- One group performs the scene while the rest of the class calls out advice, suggestions, or warnings to the characters. The suggestions should be given to the characters in role, rather than as actors (for example, 'Watch out, don't trust her!' rather than 'Say your line more loudly').

Classroom tips

- This works best performed 'in the round' (i.e. with the actors in the middle of the audience).

- You may need to give students time to work in pairs or as a group to think about what they would shout out.

- For noisier classes, give groups time to work out what they will shout and make one person in each group responsible for their group's interruptions.

- To control things even further, you could give each group a maximum number of times they can call out – asking them to discuss which would be their three most crucial interruptions and giving them a card to hand in to the teacher each time they interrupt.

54. Using Stage Directions

AGE	11-18
TIME	1-2 lessons
GROUPING	Pair or small group work
IN BRIEF	**Students are given dialogue without the stage directions, or stage directions without dialogue and are asked to invent the missing text.**
GOOD FOR	• Lifting a drama text off the page, so that students begin to visualise it as performance. • Understanding the importance of action in drama as well as words.
RESOURCES	A pre-prepared drama extract with the stage directions deleted.
ON CD ROM	*Studying All My Sons; KS2 English and Literacy Pack; Much Ado About Nothing – an EMC Study Guide*

Activity

- Choose a key moment in a drama text, or a moment where a lot is happening in terms of action, or emotional conflict. Delete all the stage directions and ask students to write them. (You could leave gaps where the playwright wrote directions, for students to fill in, or delete all reference to the stage directions, so that students choose where to add them.)

- Ask students to swap with another pair or small group and perform the scene, according to the stage directions they have been given.

- As a whole group, talk about the differences between the performances created by each set of stage directions.

- Read the stage directions written by the playwright and talk about how they differ from the ones the students wrote.

Variations

- Reverse the activity, by giving students just the stage directions for the next scene in the play they are studying and asking them to write the dialogue to go with it. They could act out the scene, as written by different groups of students, before performing the scene in the play itself.

- Apply the same process to a screenplay extract in order to explore the visual impact of camera, mise-en-scène and movement on the action of the scene.

Classroom tips

- Writing the stage directions can be completed in a single lesson, with the focus being on students trying out different performances.

- If you are asking students to write the text itself, you will need longer – perhaps a writing lesson followed by a performance lesson, at the end of which students compare their text with the play itself.

55. The Wall of Possibility

AGE	11-18
TIME	40-50 minutes
GROUPING	Individual and whole class
IN BRIEF	**Students create a still picture to show their interpretation of a character at a particular moment in the play, and then how that character would like to be.**
GOOD FOR	• Prompting discussion about character development. • Exploring the gap between a character's outward appearance and evidence of inner thoughts and feelings. • Looking at characters' motivations.
RESOURCES	
ON CD ROM	*Richard III – an EMC Study Guide*

Activity

■ Students discover how the activity works by first creating a statue of themselves as they are now – a statue which sums up their current state of mind.

■ Give students a short time to think, then count down to a 'freeze'.

■ Choose a few students at a time to 'unfreeze' from their statue so they can look at some of the other statues.

■ Ask a couple of students to choose someone whose statue they found interesting or confusing and ask that person to take up their position again. Discuss as a group: what can you tell? How do you know? (The 'statue', of course, cannot speak!)

■ Students move through the 'wall of possibility' (an imaginary line down the centre of the room) and create a new statue to show how they would like to be.

■ Now repeat the activity with a character from the text. Begin by picking a moment in the text and asking how the character is at this point. Then, moving through the 'wall of possibility', ask how would they like to be?

■ De-brief the activity with students, exploring what they have learned about the character.

Variations

■ The activity can also be used to study characters in novels, stories or moving-image narratives.

Classroom tips

■ Let students know in advance that they will not be asked to explain the preliminary statue of themselves – this is all about the audience's reading of it. This both reduces anxiety and makes students think harder about how to put across their ideas without speech.

56. The Irony Inspectors

AGE	11-18
TIME	40-50 minutes
GROUPING	Whole class
IN BRIEF	**An activity to do while reading a scene, highlighting moments of dramatic irony.**
GOOD FOR	• Making possible audience responses explicit. • Drawing out moments of dramatic irony.
RESOURCES	A scene, taken from the set text, that contains several examples of dramatic irony.
ON CD ROM	*Richard III – an EMC Study Guide*

Activity

■ Ensure students have a good understanding of the term 'dramatic irony', for example:

'Dramatic irony is where the audience knows more about what's happening than a character does or can foresee what's going to happen. The audience therefore feels aware of the inadequacy of the character's words and viewpoint.'

■ Appoint four or five 'irony inspectors'. They will need a signal such as clapping, making a sound, ringing a bell or raising a hand to interrupt the action when they spot a moment of dramatic irony.

■ Read the scene as a class, stopping when one or more of the irony inspectors gives their signal.

■ When the action has been interrupted, you can either keep the flow of reading by marking your copy of the text to come back to when the scene is finished, or you can ask the inspector/s to explain there and then what they spotted and why it is ironic.

Variations

■ Ask the class to discuss the possible reason for the inspectors' interruptions, before the inspectors' explanations.

■ Ask students to imagine that the audience can shout out a warning or some advice to one or more of the characters onstage at this point. Decide what the audience might say.

■ Students could go on to write a paragraph or two about the use of dramatic irony in that scene. Sentence starters such as the following might be helpful:

● Act X Sc X is full of dramatic irony, for example, when... At this point the audience might be thinking/feeling...

● Another example is when ... This is dramatic irony because... At this point the audience might be thinking/feeling...

Classroom tips

■ The 'inspectors' need to have a good understanding of the concept of dramatic irony for the activity to work. With younger/ less able pupils, give the inspectors time to meet together and discuss points of irony while the rest of the class practise reading the scene. The inspectors can then work as a group during the reading of the scene.

■ Instead of reading the scene as a class, a group could perform/read it, with the rest of the class acting as irony inspectors, able to interrupt the action with an agreed signal.

Private Reading

And why not try...

You may also find the following activities useful:

Poetry:

57. Purposeful Reading Logs

AGE	11-16
TIME	15-50 minutes
GROUPING	Individual
IN BRIEF	**Prompts to support individual writing about wider or private reading in a diary or log.**
GOOD FOR	• Stopping students from re-telling the plot in their reading logs/diaries. • Moving students towards independent critical thinking about what they are reading.
RESOURCES	Reading logs
ON CD ROM	Extra Allsort – differentiated reading logs

Activity

■ Rather than leaving students to write whatever they like, or asking them to do endless book reviews, try giving students a series of prompt questions, sentence starters and more substantial assignments to choose from.

■ Provide prompts at three different levels (see suggestions on CD ROM) to encourage progression and deeper thought. Stick the prompts into the front of students' books, encouraging them to tick off each prompt or activity as they complete it to ensure they try a variety of responses.

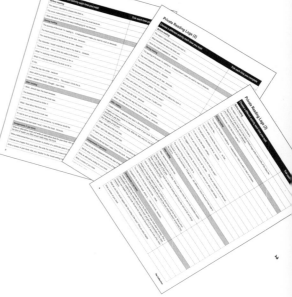

Classroom tips

■ There is a fine balance between logs becoming boring busy work and a really good way of logging thinking. Don't overdo it!

58. Class Book Groups

AGE	11-18
TIME	Several weeks
GROUPING	Individual and group
IN BRIEF	**Organise your class into several book groups who can support each other with reading.**
GOOD FOR	• Getting students to support each other in independent reading. • Promoting discussion about books. • Generating recommended books for other students or classes.
RESOURCES	A set of the same book for each group. If resourcing is an issue, you could break up sets of class readers or ask if your local library would be willing to lend sets of books.
ON CD ROM	Extra Allsort – exemplar posters

Activity

- Explain to the class how a book group works: a group of people read the same book and meet to discuss it.

- Organise the class into book groups.

- Give group guidelines, as suggested here.

  - The first half of each lesson should be spent in discussion, the second half in reading.

  - Groups set their own reading homework. They will be told in advance how long they have to read the book and will need to work out roughly how many chapters they need to read each week.

  - Each week a different person will be Chairperson. Their job is to prepare a question or a statement which could start the discussion and to take the Chair. They will also set the week's homework. That week's Chairperson has a responsibility to fill in what was missed for anyone who was absent.

- Once they have read the book, each group should create an attractively presented pack for the group or individual who reads this book next. The pack should include:

- a brief review

- an agreed group score out of 10 for the book, with an explanation

- a quote about the book from each group member

- five questions that would provoke an interesting discussion about the book

- a list of books with a similar theme or character, or of the same genre which this group would recommend.

Variations

- Advanced level students can work in this way on a set text or on wider reading and can be encouraged to share email addresses or set up blogs or MySpace pages to support each other with homework.

Classroom tips

- Groups could be of the same ability, similar reading interests or friendship groups. It can be difficult to find a book to suit everyone in mixed ability groups, although it can provide a supportive context for stretching and extending less able students' reading.

Essay and Non-Fiction Writing

And why not try...

You may also find the following activities useful:

59. What I Want to Say is This

AGE	11-18
TIME	10-15 minutes
GROUPING	Pairs or small groups
IN BRIEF	**Students tell each other the main gist of an essay before they start to write it.**
GOOD FOR	• Helping students to articulate their thoughts before writing • Encouraging students to have an overview of a piece of writing • Critical writing or non-fiction genres such as argument, where sorting out your ideas first is important
RESOURCES	
ON CD ROM	

Activity

■ Give students a bit of time to think about the title or topic and what they want to write, what angle they are going to take and what their main argument is.

■ Students have two or three minutes to tell each other, 'What I want to say is this...' They try to sum up the main things they want to get across in their piece of writing.

■ Their partner, or the others in the group, can question them about what they're going to write.

■ Students then move into a more detailed plan before starting to write.

Classroom tips

■ You could model this very briefly for students, for instance telling them just a bit of what you would say if you were doing an essay on the topic.

60. Three Endings

AGE	11-18
TIME	30-40 minutes
GROUPING	Whole class, individual and pair
IN BRIEF	**Practising endings to any genre of writing.**
GOOD FOR	• Focused redrafting. • Discussion about what makes a good ending. • Improving students' writing of endings.
RESOURCES	Several short texts with good endings in the genre under discussion, plus one piece of writing in the same genre with the ending removed.
ON CD ROM	

Activity

■ Ask students to look at several texts in the genre under discussion and talk about which endings work best.

■ As a class, make a list of effective techniques for endings, including different types of ending (e.g. summing everything up, leaving a question in the mind of the reader and so on).

■ Give students a piece of writing with the ending missing.

■ Ask students to use some of the 'effective techniques' to write three different possible endings to the piece. A more able class could be asked to write five endings.

■ In pairs, students discuss similarities and differences between their endings and talk about which ones work best and why.

■ Ask students to read out their partner's ending if they thought it was effective and explain why.

■ Show and discuss the original ending to the piece, drawing out similarities and differences with those written by the class.

Variations

■ Students can be asked to bring in examples as part of a homework preparing for the lesson.

■ Use what the students have learned to draw up a list of 'Ending' strategies a writer might employ, with particularly successful examples chosen to illustrate each.

61. Tourists and Tour Guide

AGE	11-18
TIME	20-40 minutes
GROUPING	Pair or small group
IN BRIEF	**An active approach to apply to a first draft of an essay, to help students to structure and signpost their argument.**
GOOD FOR	• Making explicit the need for signposting and clear structure. • Helping students to find tegies for signposting. • Highlighting points in a draft where more work needs to be done.
RESOURCES	First drafts of an argument or literature essay.
ON CD ROM	

Activity

- Students work in pairs or threes, looking at each person's essay in turn.

- The writer of the essay acts in the role of tourist guide. The other student(s) are tourists, who are dependent on their guide.

- The writer starts by reading aloud the first few sentences of the essay and stopping to explain what's happening, as if a tourist guide. For instance: 'Here, ladies and gentlemen, you will find an introductory sentence, explaining my main argument.'

- The tourists are free to interrupt the reading at any point with a question. For instance:

  - I'm lost. Can you tell me where we are?

  - Can you explain what's happening?

  - Can you give me an example?

  - Where are we going next?

  - Where have we just been?

- The writer should mark on the draft every point where the tourists say they're lost or want more guidance or examples.

- After the activity, share ideas about ways of signposting the line of argument in an essay (topic sentences, summing up, numbering points, introducing the next point, referring back to the title and so on). Pool some connectives and sentence starters that might help students to signpost their essay.

- Students re-draft their essay, focusing particularly on the places where they've noted elements of doubt or confusion.

Variations

- You could find other metaphors or role-play approaches to the idea of guiding a reader through a well-structured essay, for example: a guided walk through a forest; a road map, or SATNAV; the essay recipe.

- As an alternative, or next step, students could annotate their essays in the margin, explaining what they're doing at each stage.

Classroom tips

- Time the activity so that each student has a short time for his/her essay – not necessarily working through the whole thing.

- Model the process with a confident student, with you taking on one of the tourist roles.

- You could do the activity as a whole class, focusing on one essay, with the text on the interactive whiteboard and inviting different 'tourists' to come up to ask questions.

62. Writing Flow Chart

AGE	13-18
TIME	1-2 hours
GROUPING	Pair, whole class
IN BRIEF	**Students map the structure of a piece of writing and then use this as a model for their own writing.**
GOOD FOR	• Looking at the underlying structure of a piece of writing. • Moving from very scaffolded to more independent writing. • Supporting students in trying different ways of structuring their writing.
RESOURCES	A model essay or other type of writing, with the paragraphs numbered, one copy per pair. A blank writing flow chart, with a numbered box for each paragraph, joined by arrows; a further essay title.
ON CD ROM	

Activity

■ Read the essay, or other model text, together.

■ As a class, decide what the first paragraph is doing, for example 'This paragraph is setting out how this person has decided to approach the question. It also makes clear which poems the writer has chosen to compare.' Ensure students understand that they are looking for what job the paragraph is doing, rather than noting the content.

■ In pairs, students continue to map the piece of writing, noting in each box what the corresponding paragraph seems to be doing.

■ Share observations as a class. Allow time for students to add to their notes.

■ Give students the title for their own piece of writing.

■ In pairs, students use the flow chart as paragraph-by-paragraph instructions for their own piece.

■ Debrief with a discussion about which elements of the flow chart helped or hindered their own writing.

63. Simplifying Sentences

AGE	11-18
TIME	10-40 minutes
GROUPING	Whole class or small group
IN BRIEF	**Simplifying sentences from an essay to teach clarity of expression.**
GOOD FOR	• Focused work on essay writing style. • Helping students to get ⌐ ⌐ps with grammar in the context of their own writing.
RESOURCES	Some examples of overly complicated, or poorly structured sentences from previous student essays on the topic students are about to write on.
ON CD ROM	

Activity

■ Provide small groups with a sentence that doesn't work very well because it is muddled, poorly structured or cramming in too much.

■ Students read the sentence aloud as a first step, to hear why it isn't working well.

■ They identify ways of improving the sentence to make it clearer, and re-write it.

■ They share their suggestions for changes as a whole class and talk about ways of improving sentence structure in general.

■ Students have a go at writing a few sentences of their own on the same topic and, in small groups, help each other to improve them.

Variations

■ You could do exactly the same thing as a 'complicating sentences' activity, where you look at sentences that are too basic to allow a real development of ideas and show students how they might use additional clauses to add more.

Classroom tips

■ Avoid using writing by students in the class – choose snippets from past essays, or SATs or exam board exempla material. You can build up a little collection, adding to it as you find good examples.

■ Tackle issues about grammar along the way – this may be a good moment to sort out what a clause is, if it helps students to see why their own sentences don't hang together.

■ A first step may be to model this in front of the whole class, showing them how you think a particularly tortuous sentence could be unravelled and perhaps broken down into shorter, clearer units.

64. Student/Teacher Writing Dialogues

AGE	11-18
TIME	Variable
GROUPING	Individual
IN BRIEF	**Students write a comment to the teacher at the end of a piece of writing.**
GOOD FOR	• Establishing a dialogue about writing.
	• Putting the onus on the student to think about their writing, rather than passively looking at marking.
RESOURCES	
ON CD ROM	

Activity

■ At the end of a piece of writing, students are asked to write a comment, telling you what they were trying to do, what they were pleased with, or struggled with, what they'd like you to notice and comment on, what they need help with and so on.

■ Instead of marking in the usual way, you can respond first to their comment. Your marking might only be a response to their comment, or might take their comment as a starting-point for further dialogue.

■ Before their next piece of writing, encourage them to look back at the dialogue and see if there's anything worth thinking about.

■ Once this pattern is established, encourage students to write a comment directly to you, whenever they want to.

Classroom tips

■ If students don't want to 'spoil' their finished piece with a comment, suggest they use a large post-it note, or attach a comment with a paperclip.

■ Stress that the dialogues are private, between you and each student, so that they feel able to freely express worries about their written work.

■ Occasionally ask permission to read out one or two particularly interesting dialogues, so that other students see the usefulness of these written exchanges.

65. The Examiners' Meeting

AGE	16-19
TIME	40-60 mins
GROUPING	Small groups or whole class
IN BRIEF	**Students role-play a meeting of the examiners to write questions and mark schemes for an exam paper.**
GOOD FOR	• Encouraging students to think about the nature of exam questioning. • Taking on the mantle of examiner, to consider what would make a good answer. • Focusing closely on the words used in questions.
RESOURCES	Previous exam questions, copies of extracts from previous mark schemes.
ON CD ROM	

Activity

■ Set up the scenario that the students will be role-playing examiners deciding on questions for the next exam on a particular text or topic.

■ Pairs or threes write an exam question to bring to the meeting as a possible 'contender' for use in the exam.

■ Appoint a Chair of Examiners and ask them to conduct the meeting in which the examiners have to decide on two questions to use in the next exam. The team will need to select the best two questions, then check them against previous questions and the Assessment Objectives to make sure that they are good, fair questions. They may need to re-draft them.

■ Once the questions have been agreed, students use an example mark scheme as the basis for writing mark schemes for the two questions.

■ The meeting concludes once everyone has agreed that they have created two well-worded questions, with appropriate mark schemes.

■ Students go on to choose one of the questions to answer under timed conditions, for homework or in the next lesson.

Classroom tips

■ If you have a large class, you could have more than one group of examiners, perhaps meeting to write different parts of the exam.

66. Weighing up the Arguments

AGE	11-18
TIME	20-30 minutes
GROUPING	Pairs or small groups
IN BRIEF	**A speaking and listening activity in preparation for argument writing, in which students tip a 'scale' to show the strength of their opinion.**
GOOD FOR	• Discussing what makes an argument strong or weak. • Exploring how to indicate strength of feeling in writing.
RESOURCES	Topic for discussion; each pair or small group will need a ruler and a piece of A4 paper.
ON CD ROM	*The Curious Incident – an EMC Study Guide*

Activity

■ Students draw a triangle on the paper and place the ruler along the top of it, to represent a pair of scales. They write the topic being discussed at the top of the paper, for example 'TV should carry a government health warning'. They then write 'FOR' on one side and 'AGAINST' on the other .

■ Students take it in turns to state an opinion about the statement.

■ Their partner decides how far the opinion 'tips the balance' one way or the other. They move the ruler to reflect this. The more their partner thinks the statement persuades them, the more they tip the balance towards that side.

■ When they have run out of points, they can see which way the 'scales' are tipping. They can then draw along the edge of the ruler to record the result and compare with that of other pairs.

■ Students can go on to use the points made in discussion to write an argument piece.

■ You can discuss with them how to choose connectives to show the strength (or 'weight') of a point. For example:

● If a point is a strong (or 'heavy') one, they could use: More importantly...; A strong reason for thinking that is...; It is obvious that...; Most important of all...

● If a point does not tip the balance very far, they could use: It might be the case that...; It could be said that...; Some people might say...

● Then 'see-sawing' between points they could use: Equally...; On the other hand...; However...; Nevertheless...

Variations

■ This can also be done as a whole class activity with the scales created on the interactive whiteboard. Simply draw the shapes and use the 'rotate' function to tip the 'scale'.

■ Use this approach to discuss responses to a critic's reading of a text, or a controversial statement about a text.

67. An Essay in an Envelope

AGE	11-18 (particularly 14-18, in preparation for exam writing)
TIME	1 hour plus homework
GROUPING	Pair or small group
IN BRIEF	**Statement sorting to help write an essay.**
GOOD FOR	• Teaching exam writing. • Allowing students to focus on organising ideas in writing, rather than having to come up with the content.
RESOURCES	A list of 'topic sentences' for the essay students are working on. Present the cut-up statements in an envelope with the instructions.
ON CD ROM	*Studying AQA A Poetry*

Activity

■ In the lesson, give each pair or group an envelope. Ask the students to sort the statements into agree/disagree/don't know piles, in relation to the essay title.

■ Next ask students to choose five or six statements that they think might make the 'bare bones' of a good essay on the title set.

■ Ask students to choose one that might be their best first point, then work out an order for the rest.

■ Now ask students to look for one or two good bits of evidence that will allow them to explore the statement in more detail.

■ Students either go straight to writing, individually, or write a paragraph in their pair or group and share paragraphs as a whole class, to sharpen up the writing.

Variations

■ A more advanced variation might be to ask students to come up with their own five or six statements, rather than giving them the statements to choose from.

■ Another 'next stage' variation might be to ask students to write statements to go into envelopes for other students to sort.

■ You can vary the activity by applying the statements to the whole text, or an aspect of the text, rather than to a specific essay title.

Classroom tips

■ Statements should include some that are accurate but not necessarily relevant to the essay title, some that are contentious, some that are written at different levels of sophistication.

■ The aim should be to provide light scaffolding, rather than to create a straitjacket that results in everyone writing exactly the same thing. More able students should be encouraged to come up with their own statements, or amend the statements to reflect their own thinking.

■ You might like to colour code each set of statements, so that it's easy to collect them up at the end of the lesson and put them in their correct envelopes for future use.

■ How much you pause to share what different groups have done at each stage will vary according to the confidence and ability of your students.

Creative Writing

And why not try...

You may also find the following activities useful:

68. Writing a Poem Line-by-Line

AGE	11-18
TIME	40-50 minutes
GROUPING	Individual
IN BRIEF	**A step-by-step approach to writing a poem in which students write in response to prompts from the teacher.**
GOOD FOR	• Helping students to be more imaginative and by-pass their inner critic. • Helping less able students to generate ideas and a structure for writing a poem. • Focusing on re-drafting
RESOURCES	Pre-prepared prompts for writing, each prompt able to lead to a line in a poem and different senses.
ON CD ROM	Extra Allsort – classroom material

Activity

■ Think of a series of prompts, each one of which could lead to a line in a poem. It is helpful to incorporate different senses. (See examples on CD ROM for ideas.)

■ Students close their eyes and listen to the first prompt being read aloud. After about 30 seconds thinking time, ask them to write down the first thing that came into their minds, without talking to anyone else. At this stage, tell students not to edit or censor ideas or choice of language. Often the ideas that seem wildest are the most creative.

■ After 6-10 prompts, ask students to read over what they have noted down and underline their favourite words, phrases or lines. This can also be done with the help of a partner.

■ Students then build a poem around their favourite elements, trying to make the whole poem meet the standard of the best bits.

■ If you want to go further, discuss how to redraft a poem.

Classroom tips

■ Some students may be uncomfortable with closing their eyes in public. Ask them to find something to focus on, so that they do not look around the room and disturb others.

■ If you have some slow writers in the class, tell them that they can simply write a single word which will remind them later of what they imagined.

69. Paintings & Photos – Creative Writing

AGE	11-16
TIME	60 minutes
GROUPING	Whole class, followed by individual or pair work
IN BRIEF	**Visual images provide a stimulus for creative writing, both prose and poetry.**
GOOD FOR	• Sparking off ideas for writing, giving students a springboard and series of ways in. • Teaching about narrative through visual images.
RESOURCES	A poster of a painting, or image to show on an interactive whiteboard, or collection of books.
ON CD ROM	*KS2 English and Literacy Pack; The Poetry Pack*

Activity

- Show students a figurative painting or photograph, with one or more people or creatures represented.

- Students jot down first impressions of the painting, focusing on their ideas about:

  - Who?
  - Where?
  - What's happening?
  - What are they feeling?
  - What happened just before?
  - What's going to happen next?

- As a whole class, listen to different people's ideas about the painting or photograph.

- Students choose one character or idea to develop more fully by making detailed notes and adding in extra information (names, a family, events in their past, what's going to happen to them).

- Students write about their character, choosing the narrative voice and deciding whether the image is the starting-point, middle or the end of the narrative. The narrative voice could be the character themselves, someone else in the painting or an objective third person voice.

Variations

- Disclose the image bit by bit, using the spotlight tool on an interactive whiteboard, if possible. Students jot down words and phrases, then turn them into a poem.

- Students describe exactly what they see, using precise vocabulary and figurative language to convey the visual image as vividly as they can. They use this to write a poem or descriptive piece of writing.

- Students write thought bubbles for figures in the image, or for an observer. One of these thought bubbles could be extended into a longer interior monologue.

- Students give a title to the image. They use that title as the basis for a story or poem.

- Students explore the title of the image, before seeing the image itself. They write a paragraph, or a first draft of a poem based on that title. After seeing the image they then add to, or re-work their writing.

- If you have access to a program such as *Picture Power 3*, the image can be cropped, manipulated, annotated and so on, allowing individuals to focus in their writing on particular aspects or interpretations of the image.

Classroom tips

- It is worth trying to show a large scale version of the painting or photograph, ideally on a whiteboard, or as a poster. Otherwise have enough copies of the image for students to be able to look at it in detail.

70. What's in My Pocket?

AGE	11-18
TIME	40-50 minutes
GROUPING	Individual
IN BRIEF	**Students use the idea of what someone might have in a bag or pocket to create a character.**
GOOD FOR	• Preparing for creative writing. • Exploring how to 'show not tell' when developing a character.
RESOURCES	
ON CD ROM	*The Curious Incident – an EMC Study Guide*

Activity

■ Students think of a few details about a character, such as their name and age. They imagine what they might have in their pocket or bag that would show something about them. For example, what kind of person would have in their bag: a first class train ticket to Ascot; a champagne cork; a lipstick; an expensive-looking leather purse containing several credit cards and a betting slip?

■ Students write or draw these objects on separate pieces of paper and put them in an envelope.

■ Having created the 'pocket' or 'bag', students pass it to a partner.

■ They take out the things from their partner's envelope or bag, one by one. They try to imagine what kind of person would have these things in their bag or pocket. Students share their ideas with their partner.

■ They can then choose one of the following tasks:

● write one or two paragraphs about the character they created, making use of some items from their 'bag' or 'pocket'

● write one or two paragraphs about the character their partner created, making use of one or two items from their partner's 'bag' or 'pocket'.

Variations

■ This activity can also be adapted for use with a text being studied. Students present the bag or pocket they have created for a character to the whole class and explain their choices. This can be done as a way to explore what is known about the character, or as a revision activity in which others try to guess which character is represented and why.

■ Students assemble a bag of real objects and bring it in.

71. Ready, Steady, Cook

AGE	11-16
TIME	1 lesson, plus writing lessons and/or homeworks
GROUPING	Individual or pair
IN BRIEF	**A planning activity for writing stories, with a game element.**
GOOD FOR	• Teaching students about the way that writers craft stories, uncovering some of the essential features of a story. • Making explicit some key concepts in texts: character, plot, theme, voice.
RESOURCES	A set of story 'ingredient' cards, laminated for future use.
ON CD ROM	Extra Allsort — a sample set of story ingredient cards

Activity

■ Put the cards into separate piles. First ask students to choose from the character pile. Give them five minutes to do a brainstorm of possible details for their character.

■ Next, ask them to choose a card from the characteristics pile. Ask them to add this into their thinking about the character, their qualities and what's going to happen to them.

■ Keep adding fresh cards, until students have begun to firm up some ideas about what kind of story they're going to write and where it is going to lead.

■ Finally share ideas about possible narrative voices and structures to help them pull it all together into a story, for example will it be 1st or 3rd person narrative? Will it start at the beginning or the end?

■ Students write their story, either in pairs or individually, using the planning they have done to help them construct it.

Variations

■ As an alternative to the random selection of cards, you might let students make a choice of which cards they want from the pile.

■ You could do this like *Countdown*: students call out 'Character', 'Plot' etc. and you choose a card from the relevant pile and all the students use the same ingredients.

■ When students have tried this activity once, you might make it more complex by:

● asking them to write their own cards to add into the mix

● getting them to work individually

● setting a time limit or word-limit (for example a 100-word story).

■ Encourage students to experiment with using the 'ingredients' in inventive ways by introducing the 'cliché detectives', who go round looking for clichés and undertake 'crime prevention' by suggesting alternatives.

■ Use in conjunction with the 'Story Shape Diagrams' activity on page 71.

Classroom tips

■ Pause to share ideas as you go, so that students pick up fresh ideas from each other.

■ Use different coloured card for each set of ingredients, for example characters on pink, characteristics on green, events on blue, styles or genres on white.

72. Mini-Sagas

AGE	11-18
TIME	40-60 minutes
GROUPING	Individual, with whole class sharing
IN BRIEF	**An enjoyable, unthreatening way of setting up creative writing or creative responses to set texts.**
GOOD FOR	• Encouraging students to get writing, with a very limited number of words and a few constraints. • Encouraging students to summarise and crystallise the key aspects of the text (if used with set texts). • Generating discussion around redrafting.
RESOURCES	A few examples of mini-sagas; the *Guardian* 'Digested Reads' and 'Digested Reads Digested' can also be used as models if you're using the activity for set text work.
ON CD ROM	Extra Allsort – approaches and example; *The Poetry Pack*

Activity

■ Give students one or two examples of mini-sagas. They talk about which they like and why, and consider what makes a good mini-saga.

■ Give the class some titles and ask individuals/pairs to choose one to write as a mini-saga, using no more than 50 words, including the title.

■ Get students to brainstorm possible ideas that the title could lead to.

■ Students choose one idea that appeals or experiment with writing mini-sagas for several of them.

■ After writing, students share their stories and talk about what was most effective in a mini-saga.

■ Working with a partner, students re-draft their mini-sagas to improve them.

Variations

■ Random phrases could be taken from a newspaper, magazine, website or book to create a mini-saga title. Students could be asked to find one for themselves, as part of the activity.

■ Novels or short stories that have already been written could be turned into a mini-saga (like the *Guardian's* 'Digested Read Digested'.)

■ The process can be reversed so that students read a mini-saga written by someone else and turn it into a more expansive short story. The advantage of this is that the basic idea and structure are provided, which allows students to focus more on the telling than on the initial idea.

■ This activity could be combined with 'Story Shape Diagrams' (page 71) to put the focus on experimenting with structure.

■ Students write for 10 minutes, without the 50-word limit, but aiming to tell a complete story. They then pass their story on to a partner to read and together they could try editing it down to 50 words.

Classroom tips

■ This could be a strictly time-limited activity with a prompt such as, 'See what you can come up with in 15 minutes', followed by reading aloud and re-drafting.

Spelling & Knowledge About Language

And why not try...

You may also find the following activities useful:

73. The Adjectives Game

AGE	11-14
TIME	20 minutes
GROUPING	Whole class
IN BRIEF	**A team game to build knowledge about adjectives.**
GOOD FOR	• Revising adjectives. • Expanding vocabulary.
RESOURCES	A set of objects – preferably the real thing, but otherwise written on slips of paper; for each object, a list of two or three of the most common adjectives which might be used to describe it.
ON CD ROM	

Activity

- Check that the class is confident about what adjectives are and how they are used.

- Divide the class into two teams.

- Take two people from each team outside (preferably students who are fairly confident about what an adjective is). Show them one of the objects (or its name on a slip of paper). Tell them the three common adjectives they must *not* use to describe the object. The students now have 2 minutes to think of some other adjectives they could use to describe the object.

- Appoint an adjective inspector for each team.

- The team representatives return to the classroom (without the object) and stand in front of their team. They take it in turns to say an adjective that could describe the object. The pairs must not confer once they are in the room.

- Immediately after their team representative has spoken, the team can have one guess as to what object is being described. If they are wrong, play passes to the other team: their representative says a new adjective and they have a chance to guess.

- Meanwhile, the adjective inspectors must shout out if the opposing team's representative says a word that is not an adjective. If the challenge is correct, the team forfeit their guess and play passes to the other team.

- Five points are awarded for the first team to guess the object. New representatives leave the room and the game continues.

Variations

- Teams call out adjectives and the adjective inspectors try to gauge whether or not they apply to the object.

Classroom tips

- When guessing, the team should put their hand up if they have an idea. Either the teacher or the pair of representatives can choose the guesser.

- You can differentiate the activity through the choice of forbidden words.

74. Squabble

AGE	11-18
TIME	15-40 minutes
GROUPING	Small groups of 3-5 students
IN BRIEF	**Use the pieces from a Scrabble set to play a fast-moving word game.**
GOOD FOR	- Reinforcing work on spelling, especially patterns such as prefixes, suffixes, verb endings and so on. - Teaching about word classes or other aspects of word level grammar.
RESOURCES	Enough Scrabble sets to have a full bag of letters per group. You could make your own laminated card sets of letters if cost is a
ON CD ROM	

Activity

■ Before starting the game, turn all the Scrabble pieces face down on a flat surface in the middle of the group.

■ Tell students that words (of at least three letters) can be made in the following ways:

● from the letters being turned over with each turn

● anagrams of words which have already been made (and 'won') by other players

● by adding extra letters to any of the already formed words that 'belong' to players. To grab someone else's word you have to use every letter in the word – you can't leave any behind! But you can add as many as you like from the revealed letters on the table. As in Scrabble, you can't make a new word by adding an 's' to form a plural.

■ Students take turns to turn over a letter.

■ As soon as any player sees a word of three letters or more, he or she calls it out. That player takes the letters of the word and sets them out in front of them. The word now 'belongs' to them.

■ The player who 'won' the word starts the game again by turning over the next letter. New words can be created, added to and taken, as before. For example:

● Player 1 calls out 'heat' and takes the word.

● An 'h' is then turned over by that player and player 2 calls out 'heath' and takes the word.

● An 'l' is revealed later in the game and Player 1 notices it and calls out 'health' and takes the word back.

● A 'y' is revealed later in the game and player 3 calls out 'healthy'.

● No-one else manages to alter the word, so Player 3 ends up with 'healthy' in front of them and gets 7 points at the end of the game.

In the meantime, other words and anagrams are being made as people notice possible words.

■ The game ends when all the letters have been revealed and no-one can think of any more words to make. Even at the end of the game, players sometimes spot an anagram and take each other's words. The winner of the game is the person who has the most letters in front of them.

Variations

■ You can play 'Squabble' in a variety of different ways to reinforce different aspects of grammatical knowledge. For instance:

● Players are only allowed to make nouns.

● Players are only allowed to make adjectives.

● Players are only allowed to make words of two syllables or more.

■ To make the game easier, players can make 3 letter words. To make it harder, players can only make words of 4 letters or more. For real 'experts', 5 letters is an option.

Classroom tips

■ It is worth doing a demonstration of how it works first, using one set of letters. An interactive whiteboard which would allow you to move letters physically around the board would be ideal.

■ This is a good game for same ability groups rather than mixed ability groups, otherwise some students may become demoralised: one very quick-witted student could win hands down, without the others getting a look in.

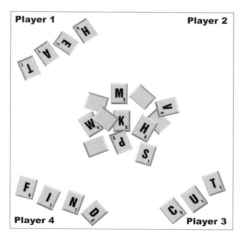

75. The Dictionary Game

AGE	11-14
TIME	10-20 minutes
GROUPING	Whole class with individual element
IN BRIEF	**Students have to guess a word from a page in the dictionary.**
GOOD FOR	• Reminding students how to use a dictionary. • Practice with alphabetical order for less able pupils. • Building vocabulary.
RESOURCES	A dictionary.
ON CD ROM	

Activity

◼ Open the dictionary at a random page.

◼ Read out the first word on the page and the last word on the page. Choose a word from the page and read out the definition only.

◼ Students try to guess what word it is, using the definition and working out which letters it must start with.

Variations

◼ This can be done as a team game.

Classroom tips

◼ The word chosen for students to guess needs to be reasonably challenging.

76. Letter by Letter

AGE	11-14
TIME	10 minutes
GROUPING	Whole class
IN BRIEF	**A quick spelling game in which students try not to finish a word.**
GOOD FOR	• Building students' understanding of letter strings as they have to try to predict what could be coming next in a word.
RESOURCES	None
ON CD ROM	

Activity

■ Explain to the students that in this game the idea is to avoid finishing a word. If a student finishes a word, he/she is out of the game (or loses a life). The finished word must be longer than three letters for the person to be out. Everyone must be aiming for a real word – they can't just call out random letters!

■ A student is asked to say a letter and the teacher writes it on the board.

■ The next person must add a letter.

■ This continues until someone has no choice but to finish the word. However, if someone suspects that a person has said a letter but does not have a word in mind (for example the letters are 'throug' and the next person says the letter 'z'), anyone may raise their hand and say 'I challenge you to tell us the word you are thinking of'. If the challenger is correct, the person they challenged is out and the challenger starts the next word. If the challenger is mistaken, the challenger is out and the person challenged starts the new word.

■ If a person is out of the game, they can still make a challenge and, if correct, get back in the game. Only the person who has just said the letter can be challenged.

Classroom tips

■ This game needs to be quick-fire to work. If it's moving slowly, you can count off five seconds per person by holding up five fingers. If they miss their turn, they lose a life or are out.

77. Top Ten Spellings

AGE	11-18
TIME	10 minutes with an individual leading to ongoing monitoring
GROUPING	individual
IN BRIEF	**Students keep a list of their 10 most common spelling mistakes. They cross off a spelling when it stops being a problem in their writing and add a new one.**
GOOD FOR	• A personalised, systematic approach to improving spelling. • Developing confidence that something can be done to improve spelling. • Improving spelling within students' own writing, rather than in isolation.
RESOURCES	None
ON CD ROM	

Activity

■ Skim through several recent pieces of work with a student. Together identify the 10 most common spelling mistakes, or spelling patterns, causing difficulty. Make a list of them, including a brief written explanation of any typical patterns. Ask the student to read through the list before starting any new piece of work and bear them in mind while writing.

■ In subsequent pieces of work, when the student stops making that particular mistake, cross the word off the list and replace it with another one.

■ Continue in this way, until the student's most common spelling mistakes have been eradicated and the list starts to include less common words.

■ Reward the student as 'milestones' are reached, for instance as two, five and 10 mistakes are crossed off.

Classroom tips

■ Since this is a personalised approach to spelling, setting it up requires either a short amount of one-to-one time with a student in class, or time outside of class to compile the most common spellings. However, it need not be done for every student. You could concentrate on those students for whom it seems most useful.

■ Once set up, it needs to be followed up regularly with the individual student, if it is to make any difference.

78. Turn the Cards

AGE	11-16
TIME	20-30 minutes
GROUPING	Pairs or small groups
IN BRIEF	**A game to help students to memorise spellings and definitions of key words.**
GOOD FOR	• Learning or revising the definition and spelling of key words.
RESOURCES	Sets of cards, each with a key word on one side and the definition of the key word on the other.
ON CD ROM	

Activity

- In groups of two to four, students spread the cards between them with the definition uppermost.

- Students take it in turns to point to a card and say and spell the word they think is on the other side. They then turn the card over to check the answer. If they are correct, they must show the answer as proof, and they can then keep the card. If they are wrong, the card is replaced, the same way up as before, without anyone else being shown the answer.

- This continues until the cards have all been cleared. The winner is the student with the most cards.

- The activity can then be repeated with the key words face up. This time students point at a card and give the definition before turning it over to check.

Variations

- This can also be played as a race against the clock, rather than students competing with each other. Partners take turns to be referee and timekeeper while the other person turns and collects the cards as quickly as they can by correctly guessing what is on the reverse. Individuals repeat the exercise two or three times and try to beat their own previous best score each time.

Classroom tips

- The department could collaborate to make laminated sets of cards, which can then be used many times. Alternatively, get older students to make cards for younger students or another class – this provides a real context for revising key words and saves you work. Check their definitions and spellings though, before using the cards!

- When you are playing this game competitively, similar ability groups are probably best.

79. Picture Books and Grammar

AGE	11-18
TIME	40-80 minutes
GROUPING	Whole class and individual
IN BRIEF	**Students read a book for a younger audience and explore the writer's use of sentence structure, to learn about simple, compound and complex sentences and their effects.**
GOOD FOR	• Exploring aspects of grammar in a real context.
	• Working with a simple text that allows students to see clearly the patterns that are under scrutiny.
	• Allowing students to imitate the patterns in order to become familiar with them.
RESOURCES	A picture book, ideally large-format.
ON CD ROM	Extra Allsort – exploring sentence structure in *John Brown, Rose and the Midnight Cat*

Activity

■ Students 'sit on the carpet', as they remember doing in primary school. Read the book aloud to them, ideally using a large picture book designed for classroom use. If a large version is not available, allow time to show students the pictures.

■ Students share their first thoughts and feelings about the text and what might make it pleasurable for a small child.

■ Using an interactive whiteboard or flipchart in a whole class plenary, look at the written text only and share thoughts about the nature of the language – the kinds of words and sentences used.

■ Discuss possible reasons for these choices and how effective they are. At this stage, introduce the idea of simple, compound and complex sentences, or reinforce prior knowledge of these concepts.

■ Students write the ending of the story, trying to copy the choices of vocabulary and sentence structure made by the writer.

■ They read out their endings and choose one or two to look at more closely and re-draft together.

Variations

■ As a next stage, students could write a complete text for a picture book, perhaps drawing on some wider reading of picture books, or in the context of looking at other aspects of the language of picture books, for example the vocabulary, the use of repetition, the relationship between words and pictures and so on.

■ If reading one book to the whole class is difficult, you could have small groups reading a book aloud to each other, and possibly use different books for each group. This reduces the scope for whole class teaching about sentence structures but might be good for a group who are already familiar with the basic grammatical concepts.

Classroom tips

■ Try to get a balance between teaching the ideas about sentence structure and vocabulary and having fun reading and writing a picture book. The grammatical knowledge can be brought in with a reasonably light touch.

Moving-Image Media

80. Using Genre Compilations

AGE	11-16
TIME	1 hour
GROUPING	Whole class; small group work
IN BRIEF	**Students watch a compilation of short moving-image extracts from the same genre, tracking the way media concepts are represented.**
GOOD FOR	• Identifying generic conventions and the way these can be adapted and challenged.
	• Exploring the cultural and social context of a genre and the ways genres change over time.
	• Practising comparative analysis and quoting from an audio-visual text.
RESOURCES	Five moving-image extracts from TV programmes linked by genre (for example: soap opera, police shows, sitcoms), and ideally representing the genre over time.
ON CD ROM	*The KS4 Media Pack*

Activity

■ Allocate a focus areas to each group, for example:

- Camera and lighting
- Soundtrack
- Mise-en-scène and location
- Narrative
- Audience
- Representation

■ Ask students to watch the whole compilation without taking notes.

■ Show the compilation twice more, pausing between screenings to give groups time to make notes on their focus area.

■ Give groups 15-20 minutes to discuss and organise their observations on each extract.

■ After sharing observations on the individual clips, students look for broad patterns and variations across the whole compilation.

■ Students report back on their focus area.

■ Use the observations as the starting-point for a more general discussion on how the genre has changed or stayed the same and to speculate about the reasons for this.

Variations

■ Use a compilation of extracts from a range of TV genres all targeting a particular audience, for example 11-15-year-olds. Focus on the ways each text addresses and represents the interests of the particular market.

■ Use a compilation of extracts from a range of factual and fictional genres linked by theme, for example by an issue such as homelessness, an event such as 9/11, or the representation of a particular social group. The focus here is on the ways the conventions and constraints of different genres affect representation.

■ Use a compilation of title sequences from a variety of factual and fictional genres. Compare the similarities and differences in the function and content of the titles.

Classroom tips

■ The focus areas in this activity allow for differentiation, ranging from the descriptive to the analytic or speculative.

■ Spider diagrams or charts with the focus headings on them can help in note-taking and in making connections between different concepts.

81. Listen With Your Eyes

AGE	11-16
TIME	10-60 minutes
GROUPING	Pair or small-group work.
IN BRIEF	**Students construct their own version of a soundtrack in response to viewing a short visual sequence.**
GOOD FOR	• Close focus on narrative cues. • Exploring the different ways a moving-image extract can be read and interpreted. • Exploring the significance of sound as a means of 'anchoring' the meaning of a moving-image sequence.
RESOURCES	A short moving image extract; playback facilities with the sound muted or volume turned down; shot list with space for students to add notes (optional).
ON CD ROM	*Double Take; KS3 Media Book*

Activity

■ Play the sequence and ask students to predict the genre of the extract, whether it's factual or fictional, who they think it might be aimed at and the reasons for their ideas. Then allocate pairs or groups to focus on one of the following aspects for a second viewing:

● Camera shots and movement

● Lighting, colour, visual effects

● Editing – number of shots, pace, transitions

■ As a whole class, share observations and findings. Explore how far students' predictions are supported by the visual evidence of the text

■ Using a shot list, students come up with their own ideas for a soundtrack to accompany the visuals.

■ Students share their soundtracks with the class, and compare their different interpretations of the sequence.

■ Screen the original extract with both sound and vision. Discuss differences and similarities between students' own versions, the visual cues which helped them construct their own soundtrack and the difference the soundtrack makes to the way the visuals are interpreted.

Variations

■ Ask groups to devise a new soundtrack which will change the meaning of the images.

■ Ask different groups to create soundtracks for the extract for different audiences or different purposes, for example a video diary, documentary or reality TV format.

■ Use a non-verbal soundtrack, for example an action sequence from a TV drama. Groups produce a verbal soundtrack commenting on the action, such as a voiceover from the point of view of a protagonist or a documentary narration. Discuss what their soundtrack adds and whether it improves on, or detracts from, the original extract.

Classroom tips

■ Texts which work well include trailers, TV continuity sequences, TV commercials, opening sequences, introductions to documentaries, voiceovers to TV news reports, or short films without dialogue.

■ The 'sound-writing' activity should take no longer than 5 minutes.

■ Use still images from the sequence rather than a shot list in order to draw attention to different camera shots and angles used in the sequence, and their effect.

82. Watch With Your Ears

AGE	11-16
TIME	10-60 minutes
GROUPING	Pair or small-group work
IN BRIEF	**Students are played the soundtrack of a moving-image clip and predict the visuals from what they can hear.**
GOOD FOR	• Developing listening skills. • Discussing the relationship between sound and visuals. • Identifying the aural conventions of different genres.
RESOURCES	A short moving-image extract.
ON CD ROM	*Double Take*

Activity

■ Ask students to close their eyes. Play the soundtrack once through.

■ Ask pairs or groups to brainstorm the different sounds they can hear, and the associations or effects of each, then discuss these as a class.

■ Play the extract again and ask pairs or groups to storyboard or describe in note form the different images they expect to accompany the soundtrack. You may need to repeat the soundtrack once or twice more, depending on its verbal content.

■ Students report back to the class and compare their different 'readings' of the sound. Discuss the aural cues which helped them construct their visual sequences.

■ Screen the original extract with both sound and vision. Discuss differences and similarities between students' own versions.

Classroom tips

■ Texts which work particularly well include trailers, TV continuity sequences, TV commercials, opening sequences, introductions to documentaries, TV news reports with voiceovers. Before the lesson, decide how to hide the visuals (turn the television around or mute/blank the projector screen). If there is a lot of spoken text you might want to provide a transcription as an aide-memoire.

■ Keep the storyboarding aspect brisk and time-limited, to keep the focus off artwork skills and on what the sound is doing and how it does it.

■ You may need to provide some prompts to help students discuss aspects of the sound such as instrumentation, volume, pitch, and rhythm.

Variations

■ Follow up the activity with one of these suggestions:

● Using the same soundtrack, ask groups to try and devise a new sequence of images which will change the meaning of the sound.

● Repeat the exercise with another soundtrack, this time asking groups to use it in a range of different contexts, for example as part of a children's TV programme, or a TV commercial.

- Soundbite scores: Compile a sequence of up to ten 5-second extracts of theme music from different film or TV genres. Students complete the activity as above, but also discuss predictions about genre. Start with one or two obvious themes, for example the *Jaws* or *Psycho* motifs, and then move onto more anonymous examples.

- Transcript tales: Provide students with a transcription of spoken text, for example from a documentary voiceover or a continuity sequence promoting upcoming programmes. Students annotate the transcript with suggestions for the visuals and any other soundtracks they think might be included.

- Create your own visuals: Groups produce a sequence of digital photographs inspired by another soundtrack. If you have software such as EMC's *Picture Power 3* or *Movie Power*, you can select a ready-made soundtrack and ask students to select from a bank of still or moving-image extracts to create their own visuals. This works very well if each group is asked to produce a text for a different target audience or context – thus the same soundtrack acquires a range of new and different meanings.

- As part of a language unit, use sound extracts which rely on a voiceover commentary or extended spoken introduction to analyse aspects of voice – dialect, register, tone – and structural differences between scripted and spoken language, voiceover and dialogue, formal and spontaneous speech. You could also use it to introduce or revise useful terms for analysing spoken language (see glossary).

- The software programs *Picture Power 3* and *Movie Power* both allow students to experiment with the different meanings a soundtrack acquires when coupled with different types of image.

83. Director's Commentary

AGE	11-16 (see 'Variations' on page 123 for examination work)
TIME	40-60 minutes
GROUPING	Pair or small group work, with whole class feedback.
IN BRIEF	**In role as director, students provide a commentary for a short moving-image sequence.**
GOOD FOR	• Developing awareness of the director's role in constructing meaning. • Identifying use of camera shots, framing, sound and edit points, and applying appropriate technical terminology. • Exploring different readings of the same text, and the difference between explicit and implied meaning.
RESOURCES	DVD playback facilities; a moving-image text students have already watched; a two-or three-minute sequence from the text for analysis (for example a key moment, an opening sequence establishing location, character or narrative); a planning grid.
ON CD ROM	Extra Allsort – grid

Activity

■ Screen the sequence and remind students of its place in the context of the whole text.

■ Explain that students will be providing an audio-commentary to the sequence from the point of view of the director, such as those provided as extras on DVDs.

■ As they watch the sequence again students pay attention to the decisions the director took. Provide some pointers to look out for such as camera shots and framing; pace of editing and effects; different types of sound. Students could use a grid format for note-taking (see CD ROM).

■ Re-screen the sequence at least twice more while students log their observations.

■ In pairs or small groups, students draft their commentary.

■ Re-screen the sequence for students to practice timing their commentary to fit the sequence.

■ Allow students to listen to two or three commentaries over the footage (making sure you've lowered the sound a bit), and compare their responses with others in the class.

Variations

■ Ask each small group to focus on a different aspect of the sequence such as visuals (camera shots and movement, framing, colour, lighting); sound (diagetic and non-diagetic sound, dialogue, music, sound-effects); editing (pace of cuts and transitions); performance (representation of characters).

■ Break a longer text down into sections, and give a different section to each small group. Screen the whole text back while a member of each group reads back the commentary to their own section.

■ Use a moving-image extract from a literary adaptation. Compare the different conventions and meanings of each medium, as well as exploring the process of adaptation.

■ Use with a complete, very short film.

Variations for 14-16 or advanced level Media Studies:

■ Apply the activity to students' own production work (for instance practical productions produced for coursework). Students select a sequence from their own production and produce a joint commentary. This provides useful scaffolding for the written commentary required for production coursework.

Classroom tips

■ Before screening the sequence, make sure you have timed it so that you can tell students how long their commentary should be.

■ The activity works best when students are given a fairly short time to write their commentaries.

84. How Well Do You Watch? Quiz

AGE	11-16
TIME	20+ minutes
GROUPING	Individual; whole class
IN BRIEF	**A light-touch introductory activity on a text for later close analysis.**
GOOD FOR	• Identifying the different elements of a moving-image text. • Practising close-viewing skills. • Introducing specialist terminology.
RESOURCES	A short moving-image text (two to three minutes), with 10 quick-fire quiz questions, focusing on the construction rather than the meaning of the text.
ON CD ROM	*Double Take*

Activity

■ Ask students to watch the extract as closely as they can, without writing anything down.

■ Individually or as a class, students try to answer the 10 questions, for example:

● How many individual shots are there in the extract?

● What instruments or key sounds are heard on the soundtrack?

● How many people are seen?

● How many close-ups are there?

■ You will also be able to ask questions specific to your extract drawing attention to a character's appearance, particular objects, details of the location, information given in captions, titles, credits.

■ Re-screen the extract.

■ Ask students to use a different coloured pen to fill in any gaps in their answers.

■ Focus the whole class plenary on the difference it made to see the extract for a second time. What sorts of things were not noticed on a first viewing? Why might this have been? How did repeated viewings increase their awareness of the construction of the sequence?

Variations

■ Ask students to provide their own questions, based on what they think are the key elements of the text after the first viewing. Comparing their questions may reveal different readings and understandings of the text, and raise useful questions about how they, as readers, make sense of the 'flow' of edited sound and image.

85. Re-editing the Text

AGE	11-16
TIME	1 hour
GROUPING	Pairs or groups of three
IN BRIEF	**Students create a new or shortened version of a media text as a cut-and-paste activity or using a software program.**
GOOD FOR	• Introducing concepts about editing, narrative, audience and representation. • Exploring the way editing shapes the meaning of a moving-image text. • Developing an awareness of narrative that can be transferred to written texts.
RESOURCES	A chronological series of 25- 40 images, captured from a moving-image text previously studied in class, either as hard copy or as image files to be used on computer.
ON CD ROM	*Double Take; KS3 Media Book – 'Patterns'*

Activity

■ Students work in twos or threes on one of the following tasks:

- ● Cut it: edit the sequence, while retaining its key meaning.

- ● Re-tell it: re-sequence the stills to create a different version of the narrative, with an appropriate soundtrack.

- ● Trail it: select key images to create a trailer for the original text, together with a commentary or voiceover and additional text captions.

■ Once groups have created their new text, they should prepare a brief commentary explaining their decisions and the impact they are intended to have on the viewer.

■ Groups take it in turns to presents their version of the text and commentary.

■ Use the group presentations as the starting point for talking about the way in which viewers make sense of moving-image texts.

Variations

■ Use still frames from different film adaptations of literary texts, as a focus for thinking about different interpretations.

Classroom tips

■ Even if you are using an interactive whiteboard or a software program for this activity, students often find it helpful to begin with a print copy of the images. This approach has the added benefit of slowing the process down long enough for students to focus closely on the framing, construction and viewpoint of each image.

■ The EMC *Picture Power 3* software contains 10 complete resource banks of images which can be used to prepare students for these tasks, together with a Do-It-Yourself module into which you can import stills of your choice.

86. The Technical Events Test

AGE	11-16 (see 'Variations' below for examination work)
TIME	10+ minutes
GROUPING	Whole class
IN BRIEF	**Students count the edits in a short moving image text.**
GOOD FOR	• Drawing attention to the construction of a moving image text.
	• Exploring the effect of editing on pace, meaning and viewer response.
	• Encouraging active engagement with a non-print text.
RESOURCES	A short moving-image text (for example, trailer, opening sequence, TV advert); playback facilities; a note of the number and range of edits in the extract.
ON CD ROM	*Double Take; KS3 Media Book*

Activity

■ Explain that an easy way to identify an edit is to look for a change in shot. Play the extract to the class and ask them to note down the number of edits they think it includes.

■ For the second viewing, tell students they are to bang on the desk each time they notice an edit (or change in shot).

■ Ask the class how many different edit points they noticed this time. Did they notice any changes of pace in the extract, for example, space between edits becoming shorter? What was the effect of this?

■ Screen the extract for a final time, asking students to focus on variations in the editing and the effect this has on their response.

Variations

■ Groups of students look out for specific types of edit (for example a cut, fade, dissolve, use of graphics, visual effects, change in soundtrack), each of which is assigned a different animal noise (so cuts are 'moos', while dissolves are 'oinks' and so on). The extract is screened with each group making the appropriate noise at the appropriate time – a fun and useful way of revealing the complexity of the editing process.

Variations for 14-16 or advanced level Media Studies

■ After introducing editing conventions, re-screen the extract, focusing on the ways in which different shots are used and why:

● shot-reverse-shot to represent dialogue

● the use of close-ups and camera movement to emphasise emotion

● cutting on action to give the illusion of continuous movement

● cutaway shots dropped in to disguise edit points

● parallel editing to indicate two events happening simultaneously in different places.

■ Apply the Technical Events Test to a TV commercial or music video montage. Then using a shot-by-shot series of still frames taken with screen-capture software, ask students to identify:

● different editing techniques

● the relationship between shots

● aesthetic features such as composition and framing of shots, the use of colour, visual effects, etc.

English Allsorts

Print Media Texts

And why not try...

You may also find the following activities useful:

Reading Any Text:

87. Creating a Video Poem

AGE	11-16
TIME	1 hour
GROUPING	Pairs or small groups, whole class
IN BRIEF	**Students work in pairs on computers to create an audio-visual reading of a poem.**
GOOD FOR	• Sharing different readings or interpretations. • Considering the syntax, pace, rhythm and voice of a poem. • Analysing the ways in which text, sound and image combine to create meaning.
RESOURCES	A poem; a library of images in digital form and as a print out; computers with software such as PowerPoint, ActivStudio, SmartBoard or *Picture Power 3*; interactive whiteboard or data projector for screening the completed video poems.
ON CD ROM	Extra Allsort– lesson plan and worksheet, using Blake's 'London'

Activity

- In small groups, students read and discuss first responses to the poem.

- Using the printout of images, students talk about which ones best illustrate their interpretation and draw up a shortlist for use in their video.

- Students view the shortlisted images on computer, fine-tuning their selection.

- Each group experiments with sequencing the images to reflect their interpretation.

- Once students are happy with their sequence, they practise synchronising their reading with the presentation of the images (two images per line is a good rule of thumb).

- Each group takes it in turn to present their video poem, reading the poem in time to the image sequence.

- Debrief by raising questions about:
  - similarities and differences in the interpretation of the poem
  - whether literal images or more symbolic/metaphorical ones work best with the particular poem
  - other images students might choose to illuminate the poem
  - whether the images change or open up the meaning of the poem, or, conversely, pin it down to a fixed meaning.

Variations

- Students find their own images to illustrate the poem, either researching and scanning examples from newspapers and magazines, searching Google images, or taking and importing their own digital photographs.

- The same processes can be used to construct a music video, using the first couple of verses of a lyric of your choice.

Classroom tips

- Programs such as EMC's *Picture Power 3* offer facilities for creating varied transitions, adding titles, manipulating images, cropping and captioning, allowing students to experiment with different ways of editing the sequence to create different effects or meanings.

- If using *Picture Power 3*, it may be helpful to show students how to use the storyboard programme and type in the text of the poem. This makes it easier for students to record their reading in time with their image sequence.

88. Reconstructing Front Page News

AGE	11-16
TIME	30+ minutes
GROUPING	Pairs if using a paper version, or whole class if using a whiteboard
IN BRIEF	**Students analyse the elements from a newspaper front page then re-construct the original.**
GOOD FOR	• Using visual and linguistic cues to draw out what students already know about newspaper layout and language. • Introducing specialist terminology which helps students to analyse newspaper texts. • Identifying the impact of visual conventions, presentational devices and design in making meaning.
RESOURCES	Two copies of a mid-market/compact national daily front page. Keep one copy intact. Cut up the other into its component elements and number them. Arrange the elements randomly onto an A3 sheet and photocopy for each group.
ON CD ROM	*Doing News*

Activity

■ Ask pairs to annotate each extract for content, meaning, and voice, purpose and function, and then attempt to re-assemble the components as they might appear on the original front page. They can do this very simply by doing a thumbnail sketch and numbering it to show which elements should go where.

■ Compare students' versions with the original front page. This is a useful way of introducing or revising newspaper terminology – and also of identifying the cues offered by font size and variation, the use of visual conventions such as bullets, bold or italic text, pull quotes or reversed-out text.

Variations

■ For use on the interactive whiteboard, scan in the page, crop each element and put into a separate text box. Screen each text box in turn for discussion. Ideally, they could drag and drop each component onto the appropriate space in a blank template, to construct the page.

■ To extend the activity, ask students to write a structured analysis of their given front page, showing how its selection of stories, verbal and visual language, and techniques of layout and presentation work to represent the news stories to readers.

■ Use the front pages of consumer magazines, teen magazine titles, or even web pages.

■ Offer small groups different but same-day newspapers to work on, so that they can then compare different editorial decisions, and begin to make connections between the type of coverage and the editorial values of each newspaper.

■ Ask students to devise their own front page cut-ups for other groups, including their own annotated 'master page' analysing the original.

Classroom tips

■ When you cut up the page, make sure students can't work out from the shape of the pieces where things should go.

■ The focus of the learning should be on students' understanding what each element contributes rather than on getting the right bits of the front page in the right places.

89. Change It!
Commutation Tests

AGE	11-16
TIME	15 minutes
GROUPING	Pair and whole class work
IN BRIEF	**Students experiment with altering different elements of a media text to explore the way its meaning changes.**
GOOD FOR	• Introducing more detailed practical or analytical work on adverts, posters or magazine cover design. • Exploring the connotations of design features, and the way they convey meaning. • Investigating the importance of visual choices and their impact on representation.
RESOURCES	A print advert, magazine cover or film poster, with visual image, copy (written text) and title or slogan scanned onto computer; photocopies of a traced outline of the main elements of the text; interactive whiteboard.
ON CD ROM	*Doing News*

Activity

■ Show students the original text on an interactive whiteboard and talk about the different elements and their connotations.

■ Give each student a copy of the outline text. Begin by asking each student to write the title caption in a style which is entirely different from the original (for example, if the original caption is black and a bold, sans serif font, they might choose to write it in green italic copperplate).

■ Share different versions with the class, and explore the differences each variation makes to the meaning of the original.

Variations

■ Continue the exercise by asking students to change (or commute) further elements (for example, experimenting with colour; changing the race, age or gender of people in the image; omitting or changing objects seen in the image, etc.) each time discussing the effect of the change on the meaning and impact of the text.

■ With access to computers and DTP programs, students could explore more fully and with greater sophistication the effects of different fonts, colours and visual effects.

■ The technique transfers very effectively to the analysis of websites, logos, product packaging and to moving-image texts such as TV commercials where the visual images are critical in conveying the desired meaning.

■ The connotations and emotional impact of sound can be explored in the same way, with students substituting different music tracks for an existing advert; reading a slogan, commentary or news headlines in dialect or a different register or tone of voice.

90. Here is the News

AGE	14-16 (see 'Variations' below for examination work)
TIME	1 hour +
GROUPING	Small groups, preferably fours
IN BRIEF	**Students use newspaper articles to create a three-minute commercial radio news broadcast targeting a specific audience.**
GOOD FOR	• Developing students' understanding of what makes a news item 'newsworthy'.
	• Developing skills of information retrieval, summary, drafting and editing.
	• Understanding the ways audiences are categorised, targeted and addressed by different publications.
RESOURCES	A class set of tabloid and/or mid-market newspapers for the same day; a stopwatch, for timing the final outcomes; scissors, highlighters and paper; a set of cards featuring name and audience profile for a series of fictional radio stations.
ON CD ROM	

Activity

■ Organise the class into small groups and give each a newspaper and a radio station card. Explain that they will be using the newspaper they have been given as the basis for a three-minute news broadcast for the station on their card.

■ Ask each group to agree on at least two news items which they think are of national importance. These should be genuine 'front page news' stories, taken from the early pages of their paper. Allow about five minutes for this.

■ Groups then identify four to six further news stories which they think would be of interest to their given audience.

■ Each group now works on producing a script for their radio bulletin. The script should:

  ● include the two major stories, plus others, in an appropriate sequence or running order

  ● include features, language and a mode of address which will appeal to the target audience

  ● demonstrate awareness of features of radio news bulletins

  ● last for exactly three minutes.

■ Now give groups five minutes to rehearse their broadcasts before going 'on air'.

■ Ask each group to present its broadcast to the class. Use a stopwatch to ensure that they are 'live' for exactly three minutes – if they over-run, they must stop when time is up; if they haven't got enough news, they should be told how much silence remains at the end of their 'broadcast'.

■ Debrief the activity. Points to raise include:

  ● the different selections of stories, and the variations in running orders: which stories were newsworthy and why?

  ● what assumptions has each group made about its own target audience, and how far have they met the demands of the brief?

  ● differences in styles and language of the presentations

  ● problems groups encountered in reporting on their stories, and in meeting the deadline.

  ● what students have learned about the process of selecting news stories and 'packaging' them for audiences.

Variations

■ For a longer, more challenging exercise, book the class into the ICT suite and ask them to use the BBC news home page http://news.bbc.co.uk so they can select and research their stories independently.

■ This activity could cover a variety of learning outcomes, including: the drafting and editing process; the speaking and listening skills involved; or the understanding of audience and purpose.

Variations for 14-16 or advanced level Media Studies

■ Ask groups to produce a recorded broadcast following standard broadcast conventions and using a range of sound sources.

■ For a more news-focused exercise, give each group a different newspaper to work with, and a radio station sponsored by that newspaper, so they are producing radio versions of their newspaper's editorial values. This will provide interesting comparisons when different newspaper groups compare their choices of stories and styles.

Classroom tips

■ Keep the activity going at a cracking pace, with frequent time-checks and reminders of deadlines.

91. Not Lost in Translation

AGE	11-16 (see 'Variations' below for examination work)
TIME	30-60+ minutes
GROUPING	Pairs or small groups
IN BRIEF	**A non-fiction print text is read, summarised and adapted for another medium and a specific audience.**
GOOD FOR	• Identifying the key points and overall argument of a non-fiction text. • Exploring the ways information is presented in different media and genres. • Understanding the significance of audience on the selection of information.
RESOURCES	A print article incorporating factual data and editorial comment; a set of cards, each specifying a media context, for example a radio news item, a children's TV news programme, a daytime magazine programme.
ON CD ROM	*Doing News*

Activity

■ Read the article as a whole class, using strategies such as highlighting and annotating.

■ Give each group a context card. The task is to re-present the article in a different medium for the audience and genre shown on the card. Their aim is to select what is most relevant for the context and to find creative and appealing ways of presenting the information to this audience.

■ Each group presents their approach back to the rest of the class, explaining how and why they have repackaged the material. Debrief after each report-back, focusing on the following:

● problems encountered in adapting the data for entirely different media

● differences in information selected – what has been emphasised and why

● which sources of information have been mentioned, for which audiences, and why

● what is the editorial point of view, or opinion, expressed in the treatment

● how far does the genre and audience affect the information selected.

Variations

■ Use a literary text and explore how its language and structure changes when adapted for radio, a TV drama genre, or a news report.

■ Use a moving-image extract as the starting point for a print article.

Variations for 14-16 or advanced level Media Studies

■ Revise or foreground the generic features students should apply to their given contexts.

Classroom tips

■ You need not spend long on unpicking the conventions and characteristics of the audiences and genres on the cards – a simple brainstorming exercise should be enough.

■ The timing of the activity will depend on the length of the original article, the complexity of the briefs, and the extent of 'finish' to the work, from a rough treatment to a detailed storyboard.

Media Simulations

92. The Talk Radio Debate

AGE	14-16 (See 'Variations' below for examination work)
TIME	1 hour +
GROUPING	Small group work, with whole class 'on-air' panel discussion and audience debate
IN BRIEF	**Students explore a media event, issue, or debate in role as participants in a radio talk show.**
GOOD FOR	• Engaging actively with contemporary issues or debate. • Encouraging students to consider and articulate viewpoints other than their own. • Providing a context for structured debate, developing speaking and listening.
RESOURCES	A topical media dilemma or issue for debate (see below for examples); role-cards representing the perspectives of different age groups and interests.
ON CD ROM	*Media Relate*

Activity

■ Allocate role-cards to each group. Each group prepares a 90-second presentation exploring the perspective represented on their role-card, and elects a spokesperson to represent them in the panel discussion.

■ Re-organise the class for a studio debate. The elected spokespeople sit on the panel, while the rest of the class become members of a studio audience, contributing views from their given perspective. As teacher you will play the part of the host, introducing the programme, summarising the issues, and chairing the panel and discussion.

■ Panellists give their brief presentations in turn, before the radio host opens the discussion to the floor, eliciting responses from as many audience members as possible.

■ At the end of the debate, the host summarises the main arguments and viewpoints raised in the discussion.

■ Debrief the activity. It's also worth considering 'out-of-role' issues such as how well it worked and what's been learned.

■ Write a review of the Talk Radio Debate Show, incorporating an evaluation of the arguments presented and issues raised.

Variations for 14-16 or advanced level Media Studies

■ A Media Studies class could focus in more detail on the form and conventions of the talk radio genre, analysing a compilation audiotape of contrasting extracts from talk radio before attempting the role-play.

■ This activity can be reconfigured as a practical exercise, with one group of students in role as the production team, taking responsibility for organising the timing and format of the show, scripting an introduction to the debate and participants, recording the proceedings, and scribing the key issues.

■ Re-frame the debate as a TV Talk Show, record it on video and follow up the debate with work on title sequences and graphics for the programme. This would be both a useful production experience for a Media Studies group, and a valid practical activity as part of a coursework assignment on the topic.

Classroom tips

■ Establish the 'rules' of the radio show before you start. It's helpful to define clear time-limits and an end-point, and to keep the panel presentations brisk and concise.

93. You the Jury – Debates and Dilemmas

AGE	14-18
TIME	1 hour
GROUPING	Small group
IN BRIEF	**Students explore and debate editorial dilemmas before researching how they were tackled in the real media world.**
GOOD FOR	• Providing a context for developing research skills and argument in talk and writing. • Drawing attention to the institutional constraints shaping media and news coverage. • Introducing media regulation, the reasons for its existence, and its strengths and shortcomings.
RESOURCES	Brief summaries of dilemmas faced by media producers on cards; possible solutions; summaries of the real outcomes of each case for debriefing.
ON CD ROM	*Doing News*; Extra Allsort – an example; *KS3 Media Book; KS4 Media Pack; Panic Attacks*

Activity

◼ In small groups students read and discuss the dilemma, in role as newspaper editor, TV producer etc and debate possible courses of action.

◼ They decide on a course of action and note down the reasons for their decisions.

◼ Students go on to research the 'real world' outcome and prepare a brief presentation of the dilemma, the solution they chose and the real outcome of the case.

◼ Groups take it in turns to make their presentations and the class discuss the implications.

◼ Debrief the activity by raising broad questions around media regulation, for example: why do we need it, whose interests does it serve, is it effective, what dangers does it pose and so on.

Variations

◼ Follow up the discussion with a discursive writing task to persuade, argue or advise, such as: Do audiences need protection from the media?

◼ Groups can consider more than one dilemma, allowing them to consider the range of solutions chosen and the reasons for these.

◼ You could focus the activity on dilemmas in one medium only, for example press, film or advertising.

◼ Students research and prepare dilemmas for another group to debate using the websites for the regulatory bodies, the Press Complaints Council, Ofcom and the Advertising Standards Authority.

Classroom tips

◼ Remove names of protagonists and producers from the cards, so that students focus on the principles of the dilemma before exploring its connections with real events and stories.

94. The Pitch

AGE	11-16 (see 'Variations' below for examination work)
TIME	1 hour
GROUPING	Small group work
IN BRIEF	**Students prepare and present a pitch for a TV programme for a particular audience.**
GOOD FOR	• Exploring genre conventions, similarities and differences. • Understanding the ways particular media texts are targeted at specific audiences. • Writing to persuade, argue and advise.
RESOURCES	A briefing memo from a commissioning editor for each group.
ON CD ROM	*Doing News;* Extra Allsort – simulation

Activity

■ In small groups, students brainstorm responses to the brief.

■ They choose the idea they think meets the demands of the brief most effectively and begin to draft a 3-minute presentation to give to the commissioning editor. The presentation should include:

● a brief synopsis of the proposed programme

● a brief overview of the target audience and the reasons the proposed programme will appeal

● at least two of the following pieces of documentation to support the pitch: casting suggestions; locations; storyboard of title sequence or opening scene; outline of a pilot episode; blurb for listings columns; a brief press release about the show.

■ Groups take it in turns to 'pitch' their ideas.

■ At the end of each presentation, question the group on any aspects of their pitch which need clarification or extension.

■ Students individually write up the pitch as a formal persuasive report for the commissioning editor.

Variations

■ Provide groups with different constraints, for example a low budget, a particular theme, schedule slot, format or no-go area.

■ Pitches can also be made for digital radio stations, radio programmes, films, magazines, newspapers, advertising and so on.

Variations for 14-16 or advanced level Media Studies

■ This task can be extended for older students or Media Studies groups to allow for a longer research and production period, and more fully worked-up documentation, including hands-on production, which could be used as part of a Media Studies coursework assignment on the genre.

Classroom tips

■ This activity works with virtually any media genre. Tried and tested examples include: a new TV reality show format; a new game or quiz show; a new teen magazine title; a new soap, sitcom or crime drama series.

■ A brisk schedule, with a non-negotiable deadline and plenty of time-checks will help focus group negotiation.

Media Concepts

95. How Do You Read?

AGE	14-16
TIME	15 minutes
GROUPING	Pair and whole class work
IN BRIEF	**Students observe and log each other's behaviour in reading a newspaper and develop hypotheses about the reading process.**
GOOD FOR	• Introducing a scheme of work on newspapers or magazines. • Exploring the significance of layout and design in the reading process. • Investigating how readers use newspapers or magazines, and the pleasures they offer.
RESOURCES	A selection of national tabloid and middle-market newspapers.
ON CD ROM	*Doing News*

Activity

■ Provide each pair with a copy of a newspaper.

■ Student A reads the newspaper for three minutes, while B notes down the way the newspaper is read: sequence, speed of page-turning, facial expressions, eye movements and so on.

■ A recounts to B their experience of reading the newspaper, including which stories were read, pictures or headlines which made an impact, and any thoughts which occurred while reading.

■ B feeds back their observations on A's reading process. They discuss any differences between B's observations and A's perceptions.

■ Students swap roles.

■ Students use the observation notes to map their own reading pathway diagrammatically.

■ Students take it in turns to feed back their experiences and describe their reading patterns. Use this feed back as the starting point for a general discussion about individual reading patterns, the ways different newspapers are navigated, which bits of the publication are read least and most often, aspects of layout and design which attract attention or motivate closer reading.

Variations

■ The feed back on the aspects of the publication which particularly engage students could lead to a small-scale survey about the appeal of different features for different audiences. Issues of gender and age might be also interesting here.

■ This activity also works well with consumer magazine titles, targeting a particular readership, for example women, teen girls) and with web pages.

Classroom tips

■ It is best to keep the reading time short to prevent students being sidetracked by the content of their publication.

96. How Do You View?

AGE	11-16 (see 'Variations' below for examination work)
TIME	1 homework and 1 lesson (1 hour)
GROUPING	Individual viewing, pair and whole class work
IN BRIEF	**Students log their viewing of a specified TV genre across several days, share findings and explore patterns of viewing.**
GOOD FOR	• Alerting students to their own TV watching habits through a simple diagnostic activity. • Using students own media consumption to focus on the concept of audience. • Considering how and why TV genres are scheduled, packaged and promoted to appeal to particular audiences.
RESOURCES	Viewing log
ON CD ROM	Extra Allsort – viewing log

Activity

■ A week before the start of your scheme of work, hand out viewing logs and tell students they will be undertaking primary research by watching at least one example of the genre being studied and dipping into a selection of others.

■ In class, working in small groups, students share viewing logs, then feed back the main points of their discussion to the rest of the class. Use the feed back as the starting point for a discussion on:

- the range of programmes watched

- how students view – where, with whom, what else they do at the same time

- their preferences – which examples they would/not choose to watch again.

Variations

■ This activity can be extended for another homework and lesson with groups of students allocated the task of watching a particular example of the genre and noting the circumstances and social aspects of viewing. In class, they join up with others who have watched the same programme and compare notes on they way they watched, highlighting any patterns they notice. These

are then reported back to the class, forming the basis of a general discussion.

■ An adapted version of this activity is particularly helpful in exploring a cross-platform genre such as news or advertising.

Variations for 14-16 or advanced level Media Studies

■ The data from the exercise could be used with Media Studies classes as the focus for exploring a range of other genre-related issues such as variations in format, narrative structure, targeted audience and scheduling.

Classroom tips

■ It is helpful both to send a letter home with a clear explanation of the activity's purpose and to provide opportunities for students to watch recorded programmes in school.

■ A copy of a weekly TV listings magazine is a useful stand-by; with some classes you could provide a list of examples with their scheduling details so everyone knows what's on when.

■ This activity works particularly well with mainstream fiction or factual genres such as soap, sitcom, reality TV or TV news.

97. Instant Synopses

AGE	11-16
TIME	20+ mins
GROUPING	Individual and pair work, with whole class plenary
IN BRIEF	**As a first response to a moving-image text students summarise it in no more than 25 words.**
GOOD FOR	• Drawing attention to reading as an active process, in which the reader contributes to meaning of the text. • Encouraging discussion of alternative interpretations.
RESOURCES	A short moving-image text.
ON CD ROM	

Activity

■ Show students a short moving-image text.

■ Working on their own, students write a summary of the moving image text. Set non-negotiable time (three minutes) and word limits (25 words).

■ Three or four students read out their summaries, as the focus for a whole class discussion, exploring some of the following questions.

● Do they re-tell the narrative, or summarise the theme/meaning?

● Do they refer to individual characters, or to the broader context or issues?

● What key words are used in each summary – and what do they suggest about the way the student has interpreted the text?

● How do students' readings differ – is there agreement, or has the text meant different things to different people?

■ If appropriate, continue to work on the moving-image text in more detail, according to your main objectives, using some of the other strategies in this book.

■ At the end of the study, return to students' summaries, and discuss the ways in which their reading of the text has altered and why this might be.

Variations

■ Reduce the text even further:

● a 'tagline' – the slogan (no more than 10 words) used by media producers to sell a product to audiences, for example 'In space no-one can hear you scream' (*Alien*)

● a Hollywood style-pitch, summing up in 5 words what the text is like, for example *Jaws* meets Jane Austen

● a one-line comment for the *Radio Times*.

■ This activity works equally well with a print media or literary text.

Classroom tips

■ The aim of this activity is to capture students' initial responses to the texts, so the time and word-count should be limited enough to preclude extensive reflection. The point is to compare instant, first-impression summaries with more reflective responses acquired after more detailed analysis and discussion.

98. Generic Card Games

AGE	11-16 (see 'Variations' below for examination work)
TIME	30-60 minutes
GROUPING	Pair or small group work, with whole class sharing
IN BRIEF	**Students experiment with grouping examples of a particular media genre in different ways.**
GOOD FOR	• Investigating the concept of genre and its importance to media producers. • Drawing attention to the way in which media genres develop and change over time. • Introducing ideas about intertextuality.
RESOURCES	A set of 40 cards per pair or small group, with titles representing the full range of media texts in the genre under study (for example: sitcom, police shows, hospital drama etc).
ON CD ROM	Extra Allsort – sitcom cards

Activity

■ Distribute a set of cards to each pair or small group. The cards can be used in the following activities.

- Different groupings: Students find as many different ways of grouping the titles as they can, for example by theme, TV channel, whether they have watched them, period in which they were screened and compare their groupings with the rest of the class.

- Spot the show: Pairs pick one of the titles, and in 30 seconds summarise its chief characteristics, audience appeal and style – without referring to it by name. The rest of the class must guess which title it is.

- Convention-spotting: Compile a class list of the familiar conventions of the genre, and ask pairs/groups to call out three titles which match each convention and three titles which challenge or subvert it or combine more than one genre.

- The pitch: Pairs/small groups use the cards to identify a gap in the market, for example an audience not normally addressed by the genre, or a social group, area or region not normally represented within it. They develop an idea for a new programme and prepare a pitch to a commissioning editor, producer or publisher, through reference to other existing texts. A soap opera example: a new soap targeting 20-somethings for BBC3: *Corrie* meets *Sex and the City* in Leeds.

Variations for 14-16 or advanced level Media Studies

■ This activity is a useful way of introducing the breadth and range of a genre set as an examination topic, at 14-16 or advanced level.

■ Pairs or groups identify a title they are unfamiliar with, research it online for homework, and report back to extend the class repertoire for the genre.

99. Media Detective Work

AGE	11-16 (see 'Variations' below for examination work)
TIME	1-2 lessons
GROUPING	Small groups
IN BRIEF	**In role as journalists, students use mini-case studies from industry websites, the trade press, or regulatory agencies to research and produce an evaluation of a media text.**
GOOD FOR	• Finding out more about the ways the media industries work, from the inside. • Exploring the context of texts or genres studied in the classroom. • Developing students' skills of navigation, information retrieval, and evaluation of source material.
RESOURCES	A selection of extracts from trade publications, online publicity materials, including: viewing figures or other audience data; information on the production process; the media pack or press kit; media coverage, for example reviews.
ON CD ROM	*Doing News;* Extra Allsort – research guidance

Activity

■ Use one or two of the texts to model the reading and evaluation process, drawing out the questions students might need to ask, for example:

● Where did it come from?

● Who has produced it, and why?

● What is its 'real' purpose – to inform, critique or promote?

● Who is it for?

● Is the information reliable, or can it be challenged?

● Is it objective or does the producer have a particular interest?

● Does it offer a position or point of view?

■ Before beginning their research, students choose or are allocated the form, purpose and audience of the research text they will be producing and come up with three or four questions to guide their reading of the mini-case studies. Possible content:

● a short written piece for the *Radio Times*

● the entertainment page of a tabloid newspaper or a teen magazine about the way the text was produced

● a PowerPoint learning resource for next year's class

● a web page about the text for the company which produced it.

Variations

■ Media texts aimed at teenagers (for example teen magazines) work particularly well for this activity.

Variations for 14-16 or advanced level Media Studies

■ Provide students with a list of relevant websites to allow more extensive, independent research.

Classroom tips

■ It's worth spending some time talking about and modelling the way statistical data should be read critically as students have little experience of dealing with such evidence and can often accept it unproblematically.

Media Glossary

180 DEGREE RULE

A rule used in conventional narrative editing which maintains action should be filmed from one side of an imaginary line, in the interests of continuity. So called because there should not be more than 180 degrees between camera angles in two consecutive shots.

CROSSING THE LINE

Failure to follow the 180 degree rule, by crossing the line of action.

CAMERA ANGLE

The viewpoint chosen to photograph a subject.

CLOSE-UP

Usually defined as a shot framing the head from the neck up, sometimes with part of the shoulders.

CONTINUITY SYSTEM/CONTINUITY EDITING

The system of editing usually used in mainstream cinema to create the illusion of continuity by cutting seamlessly from one shot to another without calling attention to the editing. This system includes invisible editing, eye-line matches, and cutting on action.

CROSS-CUTTING (AKA PARALLEL EDITING)

Alternation between two or more different scenes which are (usually) taking place at the same time.

CUT

A clean break between consecutive shots.

DIAGETIC SOUND

The 'natural' sounds generated from on-screen actions and objects (eg footsteps, explosions) but also by off-screen sounds that belong to the world being depicted (eg birdsong, church bells). Non-diagetic sound includes music and/or sound effects not generated by the action of the narrative but added on in post-production to create atmosphere, suggest characters' emotions or mood, or to create audience response.

DIGITAL TECHNOLOGIES

The system for recording and reading audio-visual information in computer-based numerical codes. Besides being easier to access, manipulate and store than analogue texts recorded directly onto tape, digital versions of texts are all of equal quality.

DISSOLVE OR MIX

This is when two shots are on screen at the same time, visible through each other. The first shot is faded out while the second is faded in.

DISTRIBUTOR

The distributor of a film 'property' buys it from the production compoany, then re-sells or rents it to the exhibitor. Distributors are responsible for marketing individual films or videos.

EDITING

The process by which shots are put together into sequences or scenes. Usually described according to rhythm or pace (ie the varying lengths of the shots in the sequence) and type of transition (for example cut, fade, dissolve or mix, wipe). A montage sequence is a series of shots which establishes an atmosphere or mood, or summarises an action rather than playing it out in the equivalent of real time.

ESTABLISHING SHOT

A wide shot (usually at the start of a scene or sequence) which shows the environment in which the action will take place.

EXTREME CLOSE-UP (ECU)

A very close shot filled by part of someone's face or of an object.

EXTREME LONG SHOT (ELS)

A shot showing the scene from a great distance.

EYE-LINE

The direction of a character's gaze.

FRAME

Individual still image of a film or video, or the rectangle within which the image is composed or captured.

FRAMES PER SECOND

The number of still images that pass through the camera/projector per second. Film usually runs at 24 fps, video at 25 fps.

GENRE

A term used to categorise different types of print or moving image texts. In film study, genres are traditionally evaluated in terms of recurrent visual conventions, narratives, iconography, themes, and character types, which can be tracked and compared across individual examples of a particular genre. The concept of genre is useful both to the film industry in marketing films to audiences and thus generating profit, and to audiences, for whom generic familiarity and variation, similarity and difference, creates pleasure. The concept of genre is fluid and continually changing, with the emergence of 'hybrids' which incorporate references to several genres. It can be applied to other media forms; television is also described in terms of formats, such as the gameshow or the chatshow.

HIGH-ANGLE SHOT

A shot looking down on the action.

ICONOGRAPHY

A set of visual representations associated with a media text, genre, or personality which have acquired classic or symbolic status or meaning. The iconography of *Coronation Street* includes the terraced streets, chimney stacks and the Rovers Return; punk music iconography might include the safety pin, the Mohican, bondage gear, cut and paste lettering; as a fashion icon herself, Victoria Beckham's iconography would include her trademark sunglasses, bob and heels.

JUMP CUT

A cut between two shots of the same object, character or scene which 'crosses the line' and creates the effect of disjuncture or, literally, a jump.

LONG SHOT (LS)

A wide angled shot, in which a full human figure can be seen at a distance.

LOW ANGLE SHOT

A shot looking up at the action.

MEDIUM LONG SHOT (MLS)

Normally shows the human figure from the knees up.

MEDIUM SHOT (MS)

Normally shows the human figure from the waist up.

MISE EN SCÈNE

All the elements visible within a shot - the set, the props, the actors, the use of colour and light - and the way they are composed or choreographed within the frame of the shot. Literally, 'what's put in the scene'.

MIX

See dissolve.

MONTAGE

In still images, a collection of linked or contrasting photographic images and/or text combined to form a single composite; in film or television, a sequence of linked or contrasting moving image shots edited together non-chronologically to create new meaning, atmosphere or the passage of time.

OPENING TITLES

The credits shown on screen at the beginning of a film, usually including the title, producers, directors, writer and principal cast.

OVER-THE-SHOULDER (OTS)

A shot over the shoulder of a character in the foreground of the frame, which includes the central focus of the shot - usually another character in a dialogue sequence. This is often used in shot-reverse-shot editing (see below).

PAN

When the camera remains in a fixed position but pivots from left to right, or vice versa.

PARALLEL EDITING

See cross-cutting.

POINT OF VIEW (POV) SHOT

A shot where we appear to be looking through the character's eyes, from his or her point of view.

POST-PRODUCTION

Stage of film production after principal photography, including editing, sound/music, special effects etc.

REACTION SHOT

A shot in which we see the character's reaction (sometimes after a POV shot).

SCREENPLAY

The script produced by the screenwriter of a film, rigorously formatted to indicate the timing of each scene (usually one page of screenplay approximates to one minute of film), dialogue and stage directions, but no camera or technical instructions.

SCENE

The basic dramatic unit, usually continuous in time and setting. A feature film will usually consist of 30-60 scenes, though there are wide variations.

SEQUENCE

A group of shots showing a single piece of action, for example a chase sequence. often synonymous with 'scene', but can also be part of a larger scene.

SHOOTING SCRIPT

The version of a film or TV script or screenplay used on set, complete with camera and lighting instructions, dirctor's comments, and sound cues. Usually presented in the order of the actual shoot rather than in narrative chronology.

SHOT

The basic unit of meaning in a moving image text. It can be described according to its length, or duration, the way it is framed (ie the camera distance and angle), and the arrangement of elements within it (often referred to as the mise en scène).

SHOT/REVERSE SHOT

A convention of alternating shots used in filming dialogue. One character is shown looking (often off-screen) at another; the second character is then shown looking 'back' at the first. Since the characters are shown facing in opposite directions, we subconsciously assume that they're looking at each other (the 180 degree rule).

SHOT SIZE

Refers to the size of the subject in the frame - close-up, long shot, wide shot etc.

SHOT TRANSITION

The transition between one shot and another which can be achieved by a cut, a dissolve, a wipe or another special visual effect.

SOUNDTRACK

The audio components of a film - dialogue, sound effects, music.

STEREOTYPES

The simplified representation of a character or social group, which offers immediately recognizable traits and assists the identification of characters. The term is often used in a derogatory way to criticize apparently lazy or deliberate misrepresentations of people or groups; yet stereotypes perform complex and specific functions in media texts, which can be usefully explored and challenged.

STORYBOARD

A series of drawings representing the shots involved in a sequence of moving images, and visually demonstrating camera position, shot length and transition, and soundtrack. Used extensively (but not always) in advertising, music video, and in particularly complex film sequences. A useful exercise in visualizing, pre-planning and drafting student production work, and in focusing on visual aspects of a moving image text or in adapting a print text for camera - but sometimes over-used as a teaching tool.

TELEPHOTO LENS

Lens with a long focal length and greater magnification than the wide-angle lens. Used for close-ups, or to zoom in from long-shot to close-up (and frequently over-used in students own production work).

TILT

When the camera pivots on the vertical axis to look upwards and downwards.

TOP SHOT

An extreme high-angle shot where the camera looks straight down.

TRACKING SHOT

A shot taken from a camera mounted on a dolly, tracks or other moving vehicle, in order to follow an action or reveal a scene.

TWO-SHOT

A shot showing two characters in a frame, often in mid-shot. Frequently used in domestic drama such as soap or sitcom.

WIDE SHOT (WS) OR WIDE-ANGLE SHOT

A shot taking in much or all of the action.

WIDE-ANGLE LENS

Lens with a short focal length, a wide-angle of view and less magnification than the telephoto lens.

ZOOM

The change of image size achieved when the focal length of the zoom lens is altered.

What's on the CD ROM?

What's on the CD ROM?

Allsorts (see page 151)

The 'Allsorts' folder includes extracts from English and Media Centre publications, student worksheets, further exemplification and suggested ways of using the strategies outlined in *English Allsorts*. The folder is organised into the main sections used in the text and by strategy. Not all strategies have additional material on the CD ROM. All additional materials are listed in the text as 'On the CD ROM'.

EMC_Samples (see page 157)

The 'EMC_Samples' folder includes:

- sample print material from all EMC publications, organised into genre and age range ('01EMC_Pubs_Print' folder)

- sample video materials ('02EMC_Pubs_Video' folder)

KS3Units

The CD ROM also includes the complete *KS3 Units* in pdf format ('KS3Units').

Allsorts on the CD ROM

Speaking and Listening Folder

	On the CD ROM
1. Debate Around the Room	*Great Expectations – an EMC Study Guide* – responding to Dickens' presentation of Magwitch *Talk on the Box* – arguments for and against daytime television shows *Studying The World's Wife* – responding to 'Little Red Cap'
2. Continuum Opinions	*Studying AQA A Poetry* – exploring similarities and differences *Much Ado About Nothing – an EMC Study Guide* – responding to Beatrice *The Curious Incident – an EMC Study Guide* – exploring the character of Christopher
4. Discussion Rally	Extra Allsort – 2 examples (*Much Ado About Nothing*; Homelessness)
6. Popular TV Formats for Talk	Extra Allsort – 4 suggestions

Reading Any Text Folder

	On CD ROM
7. A Reading Trail	*The Curious Incident – an EMC Study Guide* – exploring 'voice' in narrative (includes extracts) *KS3 Poetry Book* – poems and paintings on the story of Icarus (includes poems) *The Poetry Pack* – Wordsworth reading trail *Writing from Life* – annotated list of books and films on childhood
8. Opinion Chains	Extra Allsort – 4 suggested uses (*Lord of the Flies, Brat Camp, Great Expectations, Make Lemonade*) and modelled example using *Make Lemonade*
9. What's on the Agenda?	*Studying Othello* – an agenda for analysing any speech *Studying Wise Children* – an agenda for reading any modern novel
10. How to Ask Good Questions of Texts	*Of Mice and Men – an EMC Study Guide* – the 5 W's
11. Benchmarking	Extra Allsort – blank grid and comparative statements

CD ROM Contents

12. Counting Grammatical Constructions	*Studying AQA A Poetry* – 'Patrolling Barnegat' Extra Allsort – Jacques Prévert's 'Breakfast' *Studying The World's Wife* – 'The Devil's Wife'
14. Bag of Objects	*The Curious Incident – an EMC Study Guide* – Christopher Extra Allsort – 4 examples (*The Tempest, Make Lemonade, Oliver Twist,* Poems from Different Cultures for AQA A)
15. Circle of Intimacy	*The Curious Incident – an EMC Study Guide* – Christopher's family and friends
16. The Power and the Puddle	Extra Allsort – 2 examples (*The Tempest; An Inspector Calls*) *Sherlock Holmes – an EMC Study Guide* – exploring the status of characters in a selection of stories
18. Soundtrack Storyboards	Extra Allsort – worksheet, text and storyboard grid
19. Opinion Posters	*Studying Wise Children* – after reading responding to criticism
20. Just a Minute Soundbites	*Studying Spies* – Chapter 9 responding to statements
21. Shifting Tones – Colour Coding	*Studying Wise Children* – exploring the tone of the whole novel in response to short pieces of criticism *Studying The World's Wife* – analysing 'Mrs Midas'
23. Visual Representation of a Text	*Studying Blake's Songs* – i) 'London' storyboard *Studying Othello* – a visual map of the play *The Poetry Pack* – screen adaptations and collages
24. Picture Books and Critical Theory	*Text, Reader, Critic* – critical position cards
25. Newsnight Review – a Simulation	*Of Mice and Men – an EMC Study Guide* – responding to the characters in role as critics *Studying Othello* – responding to key scenes in role as critics and director *Text, Reader, Critic* – critical position cards and simulation activity discussing a set text in role
26. Writing in the Style of	*Studying AQA A Poetry* – writing a poem on a new topic in the style of one of studied poets
27. Key Dates – Contexts	*Studying Blake's Songs* – before reading speculating about the period *KS4 Media Pack* – 'Cops on the Box' before reading

English Allsorts

28. Images and Contexts	*Sherlock Holmes – an EMC Study Guide* – before reading representations of Holmes
	Of Mice and Men – an EMC Study Guide – statements, thought bubbles and original photos
	KS3 Fiction Pack – 'The Blood Bay'
29. KWL Grids	*Klondyke Kate Revisited* – 'Find it' text and KWL grid
30. The Game of the Book	*Extra Allsort – Spies* game
	Much Ado About Nothing – an EMC Study Guide – revision
	Twelfth Night – an EMC Study Guide – exploring structure
31. Zones of Proximity – Contexts	*Studying Cold Mountain* – exploring contexts
32. The Text as a Pack of Cards	*Studying Wise Children* – cards for revision, exploring the writer's craft, creating structure maps and so on
	Extra Allsort – Spies game
33. Text Transformations	*Three Modern Novels* – a film of *Beloved*
	Great Expectations – an EMC Study Guide – adapting *Great Expectations* for the stage
	Studying Arthur Miller – television adaptation of *The Crucible*
	Production Practices – storyboarding and recording an adaptation of Chopin's 'Story of an Hour'
35. Role-Play Prediction	*Great Expectations – an EMC Study Guide* – i) before reading telling a story; ii) eavesdropping Estella and Miss Havisham
	Much Ado About Nothing – an EMC Study Guide – telling Leonato

Poetry Folder

	On the CD ROM
36. Collapsed Poem	*Studying AQA A Poetry* – 'Patrolling Barnegat'
	Studying Blake's Songs – before reading 'The Divine Image'; before reading 'The Human Abstract'
	Richard III – an EMC Study Guide – before reading Anne's speech to Richard
37. Desert Island Poems	*KS3 Poetry Book* – choosing a sonnet for a radio programme (variation)

38. Getting the Rhythm	*Studying Blake's Songs* – Blake's use of rhythm Extra Allsort – *emagazine* guide to rhythm
39. Poem Shapes	*Studying AQA A Poetry* – comparing poems *KS3 Poetry Book* – sonnets *Texts in their Times* – Victorian and Modern – comparing poems
40. Reading a Poem Line-by-Line	*Studying Blake's Songs* – 'The Clod and the Pebble' Extra Allsort using Billy Collins' 'An Introduction to Poetry' and Charles Causley's 'I am the Song'.
41. Sound Patterns	Extra Allsort – classroom material and teachers' notes on 'The Clod and the Pebble' *Studying The World's Wife* – exploration of rhyme across the collection
43. Using a Poet's Words	*Studying Blake's Songs* – 'The Sick Rose' Extra Allsort – classroom material on 'Tichborne's Elegy'

Prose Fiction Folder

	On the CD ROM
45. The Digested Read	Extra Allsort – *The Guardian* digested read
47. Open the Book	Extra Allsort – suggestions for focusing on a single novel and for comparative study
48. Story Shape Diagrams	*Great Expectations – an EMC Study Guide; KS2 English and Literacy Pack; Writing From Life*

Drama Folder

	On the CD ROM
49. Cast Meeting	Extra Allsort – *Richard III* example *Pre-1770 Drama – Elizabethan and Jacobean – The Duchess of Malfi*
50. Cheering and Groaning Summary	Extra Allsort – classroom material on *Much Ado About Nothing – an EMC Study Guide* *Richard III – an EMC Study Guide*
51. Conversation Analysis	*Studying Othello* – exploring power relations (Othello and Iago) *Richard III – an EMC Study Guide* – analysing the conversation between Richard and Anne

52. Looking at the Cast List	*Much Ado About Nothing – an EMC Study Guide* – before reading speculating about the play *Studying Wise Children* – exploring the dramatis personae
53. The Panto Audience	*Much Ado About Nothing – an EMC Study Guide* – telling Leonato, an improvisation
54. Using Stage Directions	*Studying All My Sons* – i) the grammatical features; ii) before reading a scene – completing the stage directions *KS2 English and Literacy Pack* – exploring and writing stage directions *Much Ado About Nothing – an EMC Study Guide* – stage directions to speculate about a scene
55. The Wall of Possibility	*Richard III – an EMC Study Guide* – an activity exploring the whole play
56. The Irony Inspectors	*Richard III – an EMC Study Guide* – Act 3 Scene 4 – what Hastings does not understand

Private Reading Folder

	On the CD ROM
57. Purposeful Reading Logs	Extra Allsort – differentiated reading logs
58. Class Book Groups	Extra Allsort – exemplar posters

Essay and Non-Fiction Writing Folder

	On the CD ROM
66. Weighing up the Arguments	*The Curious Incident – an EMC Study Guide*
67. An Essay in an Envelope	*Studying AQA A Poetry*

Creative Writing Folder

	On the CD ROM
68. Writing a Poem Line-by-Line	Extra Allsort – classroom material
69. Paintings & Photos – Creative Writing	*KS2 English and Literacy Pack* *The Poetry Pack*
70. What's in my Pocket?	*The Curious Incident – an EMC Study Guide*
71. Ready, Steady, Cook	Extra Allsort – story writing ingredient cards
72. Mini-Sagas	Extra Allsort – approaches and example *The Poetry Pack* – writing mini-sagas using key words from a poem before reading

Spelling and Knowledge About Language Folder

	On the CD ROM
79. Picture Books and Grammar	Extra Allsort – exploring sentence structure in *John Brown, Rose and the Midnight Cat*

Moving-Image Media Folder

	On the CD ROM
80. Using Genre Compilations	*KS4 Media Pack* – 'Cops on the Box'
81. Listen With Your Eyes...	*Double Take* – 'Dipper'
	KS3 Media Book – 'Home Away from Home'
82. Watch With Your Ears...	*Double Take* – 'After Refuge'
83. Director's Commentary	*Extra Allsort* – grid
84. How Well do you Watch? Quiz	*Double Take* – 'Sold'
85. Re-editing the Text	*Double Take* – i) 'Dipper'; ii) 'Gravity'
	KS3 Media Book – 'Patterns'
86. The Technical Events Test	*Double Take* – i) 'Dipper'; ii) 'Dipper'
	KS3 Media Book – 'Home Away from Home'

Print Media Texts Folder

	On the CD ROM
87. Creating a Video Poem	*Extra Allsort* – lesson plan and worksheet using Blake's 'London'
88. Reconstructing Front Page News	*Doing News* – 'Reading Prince Harry'
89. Change it! Commutation Tests	*Doing News* – Photographs and captions
91. Not Lost in Translation	*Doing News* – 'Handling Harry – the TV Report'

Media Simulations Folder

	On the CD ROM
92. The Talk Radio Debate	*Media Relate* – 'Argument Show' role-play
93. You the Jury – Debates & Dilemmas	*Doing News* – Debating the role of the news
	Extra Allsort – an example
	KS3 Media Book – 'Big Brother'
	KS4 Media Pack – Teenzines
	Panic Attacks – exploring violence
94. The Pitch	*Doing News* – simulation
	Extra Allsort – worksheets

Media Concepts Folder

	On the CD ROM
95. How Do You Read?	*Doing News* – i) researching reading habits; ii) reading online
96. How Do You View?	*Extra Allsort* – viewing log
98. Generic Card Games	*Extra Allsort* – sitcom cards
99. Media Detective Work	*Doing News* – research
	Extra Allsort – research guidance

EMC_Samples on the CD ROM

01. Sample print material from all EMC publications, organised into genre and age range

02. Video material from EMC publications

Sample Print Material
('01EMC_Pubs_Print' Folder)

01KS3 Series

KS2 English and Literacy Pack

KS3 Drama Book

KS3 Fiction Pack

KS3 Media Book

KS3 Non-Fiction Book

KS3 Poetry Book

KS3 Units

ShazKaz – an anthology of original short stories

02EMC Advanced Series

3 Modern Novels

Studying All My Sons

Studying Cold Mountain

The Modern Novel

Studying Othello

Pre-1770 Drama – Elizabethan and Jacobean

Studying Blake's Songs

Texts in their Times – Victorian and Modern

Studying Wise Children

Studying The World's Wife

03Study Guides

3 Modern Novels

Studying AQA A Poetry

The Curious Incident – an EMC Study Guide

Great Expectations – an EMC Study Guide

Of Mice and Men – an EMC Study Guide

Sherlock Holmes – an EMC Study Guide

Writing from Life

04Poetry

Studying AQA A Poetry

KS3 Poetry Book

The Poetry Pack

Poetry Posters 3

Studying Poetry

05Drama

Twelfth Night – an EMC Study Guide

Studying All My Sons

An Inspector Calls

KS3 Drama Book

Much Ado About Nothing – an EMC Study Guide

Studying Othello

Pre-1770 Drama – Elizabethan and Jacobean

Richard III – an EMC Study Guide

06Media

Doing News

Junk

KS3 Media Book

KS4 Media Pack

MediaRelate

Movie Power – Print materials

Panic Attacks

Picture Power 3 – Print materials

Talk on the Box

07Non-Fiction

Beautiful Game

Klondyke Kate Revisited

KS3 Non-Fiction Book

Language Works – Draft

Talk on the Box

08Shakespeare

Twelfth Night – an EMC Study Guide

Much Ado About Nothing – an EMC Study Guide

Studying Othello

Richard III – an EMC Study Guide

09MultiMedia

Movie Power – Print materials

Picture Power 3 – Print materials

Sample Video Material
('02EMC_Pubs_Video' Folder)

01KS3 Series

KS3 Drama Book – 1. Hannah and Hanna

KS3 Drama Book – 2. Helmet

KS3 Media Book – 'Juice Up' advert

KS3 Poetry Book – 1. John Agard

KS3 Poetry Book – 2. John Hegley

02EMC Advanced Series

Studying Blake's Songs – Allen Ginsberg reads 'The Tyger'

Studying Othello – 1. Critic

Studying Othello – 2. Actor

The Modern Novel – Interview with Ian McEwan

03Study Guides

The Curious Incident – Interview with Mark Haddon

04Poetry

Studying Blake's Songs – Allen Ginsberg reads 'The Tyger'

KS3 Poetry Book – 1. John Agard

KS3 Poetry Book – 2. John Hegley

05Drama

KS3 Drama Book – 1. Hannah and Hanna

KS3 Drama Book – 2. Helmet

Studying Othello – 1. Critic

Studying Othello – 2. Actor

06Media

Doing News

Double Take

KS3 Media Book – 'Juice Up' advert

KS4 Media Pack – 'Bait'

Movie Power Guide

Picture Power 3 Guide

07Non-Fiction

Language Works – Montage

08Shakespeare

Studying Othello – 1. Critic

Studying Othello – 2. Actor

09MultiMedia

Movie Power Guide

Picture Power 3 Guide